T0301931

An Analysis of

Joan Wallach Scott's

Gender and the Politics of History

Pilar Zazueta
with
Etienne Stockland

Routledge
Taylor & Francis Group

LONDON AND NEW YORK

Published by Macat International Ltd
24:13 Coda Centre, 189 Munster Road, London SW6 6AW.

Distributed exclusively by Routledge
2 Park Square, Milton Park, Abingdon, Oxon OX14 4RN
605 Third Avenue, New York, NY 10017

Routledge is an imprint of the Taylor & Francis Group, an informa business

www.macat.com
info@macat.com

Cataloguing in Publication Data
A catalogue record for this book is available from the British Library.
Library of Congress Cataloguing-in-Publication Data is available upon request.
Cover illustration: Etienne Gilfillan

ISBN 978-1-912302-75-8 (hardback)
ISBN 978-1-912128-66-2 (paperback)
ISBN 978-1-912281-63-3 (e-book)

CONTENTS

THE MACAT LIBRARY

The Macat Library is a series of unique academic explorations of seminal works in the humanities and social sciences – books and papers that have had a significant and widely recognised impact on their disciplines. It has been created to serve as much more than just a summary of what lies between the covers of a great book. It illuminates and explores the influences on, ideas of, and impact of that book. Our goal is to offer a learning resource that encourages critical thinking and fosters a better, deeper understanding of important ideas.

Each publication is divided into three Sections: Influences, Ideas, and Impact. Each Section has four Modules. These explore every important facet of the work, and the responses to it.

This Section-Module structure makes a Macat Library book easy to use, but it has another important feature. Because each Macat book is written to the same format, it is possible (and encouraged!) to cross-reference multiple Macat books along the same lines of inquiry or research. This allows the reader to open up interesting interdisciplinary pathways.

To further aid your reading, lists of glossary terms and people mentioned are included at the end of this book (these are indicated by an asterisk [*] throughout) – as well as a list of works cited.

Macat has worked with the University of Cambridge to identify the elements of critical thinking and understand the ways in which six different skills combine to enable effective thinking.
Three allow us to fully understand a problem; three more give us the tools to solve it. Together, these six skills make up the **PACIER** model of critical thinking. They are:

ANALYSIS – understanding how an argument is built
EVALUATION – exploring the strengths and weaknesses of an argument
INTERPRETATION – understanding issues of meaning

CREATIVE THINKING – coming up with new ideas and fresh connections
PROBLEM-SOLVING – producing strong solutions
REASONING – creating strong arguments

To find out more, visit **WWW.MACAT.COM.**

CRITICAL THINKING AND *GENDER AND THE POLITICS OF HISTORY*

Primary critical thinking skill: ANALYSIS
Secondary critical thinking skill: PROBLEM-SOLVING

Joan Scott's work has influenced several generations of historians and helped make the topic of gender central to the way in which the discipline is taught and studied today. At root a new way of conceptualizing capitalist societies, Scott's theories suggest that gender is better understood as a social construct than as a biological fact.

Scott's original contribution to the debate, however, stems in her use of the critical thinking skill of analysis to understand how the arguments of earlier generations of historians were built in order to fully grasp both their structure and the assumptions that underpinned them. From there, Scott was able to use problem-solving to resolve the issues that emerged from her analysis, asking productive questions focused on better ways to build a model capable of explaining the historical phenomenon of gender difference.

Scott answered these questions by introducing models created by deconstructionist scholars – notably Jacques Derrida, who challenged the idea that any term or concept has a stable or dependable meaning rooted in material reality. She was able, in consequence, to refute that idea that gender inequality is the natural (hence justifiable) consequence of biological sexual differences, and issue a fundamental challenge to the capitalist system itself.

ABOUT THE AUTHOR OF THE ORIGINAL WORK

Much-honored American historian **Joan Wallach Scott** was born in New York City in 1941. A specialist on the history of France, she is particularly noted for her original approach to historical analysis that draws on methods taken from contemporary literary theory. Treating history as a form of literary narrative, she questions categories such as gender and ideas of objective "truth" in historical research. Scott's work has played a significant role in changing the methods and aims in the field of women's history.

ABOUT THE AUTHORS OF THE ANALYSIS

Dr Pilar Zazueta holds a PhD in history from Columbia University. She is currently a lecturer at the Teresa Lozano Lond Institute of Latin American Studies at the University of Texas, Austin, where her research focuses on gender and the history of food and nutrition public policy in twentieth-century Mexico.

Etienne Stockland is researching a PhD in environmental history at Columbia University. He has taught at Columbia and at Sciences-Po.

ABOUT MACAT

GREAT WORKS FOR CRITICAL THINKING

Macat is focused on making the ideas of the world's great thinkers accessible and comprehensible to everybody, everywhere, in ways that promote the development of enhanced critical thinking skills.

It works with leading academics from the world's top universities to produce new analyses that focus on the ideas and the impact of the most influential works ever written across a wide variety of academic disciplines. Each of the works that sit at the heart of its growing library is an enduring example of great thinking. But by setting them in context – and looking at the influences that shaped their authors, as well as the responses they provoked – Macat encourages readers to look at these classics and game-changers with fresh eyes. Readers learn to think, engage and challenge their ideas, rather than simply accepting them.

'Macat offers an amazing first-of-its-kind tool for interdisciplinary learning and research. Its focus on works that transformed their disciplines and its rigorous approach, drawing on the world's leading experts and educational institutions, opens up a world-class education to anyone.'

Andreas Schleicher
Director for Education and Skills, Organisation for Economic Co-operation and Development

'Macat is taking on some of the major challenges in university education … They have drawn together a strong team of active academics who are producing teaching materials that are novel in the breadth of their approach.'

Prof Lord Broers,
former Vice-Chancellor of the University of Cambridge

'The Macat vision is exceptionally exciting. It focuses upon new modes of learning which analyse and explain seminal texts which have profoundly influenced world thinking and so social and economic development. It promotes the kind of critical thinking which is essential for any society and economy. This is the learning of the future.'

Rt Hon Charles Clarke, former UK Secretary of State for Education

'The Macat analyses provide immediate access to the critical conversation surrounding the books that have shaped their respective discipline, which will make them an invaluable resource to all of those, students and teachers, working in the field.'

Professor William Tronzo, University of California at San Diego

WAYS IN TO THE TEXT

KEY POINTS

- Joan Wallach Scott is an American historian. Her work has been influential for its analysis of the role gender has played in the formation of societies.

- According to Scott, gender definitions—what is "masculine" and what is "feminine," for example—are more rooted in society than in nature, and gender has been used to establish hierarchies of status and wealth.

- *Gender and the Politics of History* played an important part in changing the aims and methods of the field of women's history, and demonstrated that literary theory could be very useful in the analysis of history.

Who Is Joan Wallach Scott?

Scott is an American historian particularly noted for her influential works that deal with gender and history, theories of the nature of gender, and the history of ideas. She was born in New York City in 1941 and grew up in a politically left-wing family. Her parents, both teachers, were committed to social issues. In the anti-communist* climate of the United States during the Cold War,* her father, a member of the Teachers Union, was forced to resign because of his Marxist* views.

From this formative environment, Scott began her academic career as a social historian* writing from a feminist* perspective. Later, she adopted the critical techniques and theoretical approaches associated with intellectual currents like poststructuralism*—an approach to analysis that challenges the idea that there is a single "correct" reading or interpretation.

Scott applied poststructuralist methods to the analysis of gender in history, eventually writing the influential paper "Gender: A Useful Category of Historical Analysis." It was instrumental in developing "gender history" as an academic field in its own right. Her work has played a significant role in changing the methods and aims of the field of women's history.

Today, Joan Wallach Scott's reputation is secure. She is considered a historian of exceptional analytical clarity whose theoretical approach has had a notable influence in her discipline. Currently the Harold F. Linder Professor at the School of Social Science in the Institute for Advanced Study at Princeton University in New Jersey, her contributions to her academic field have been recognized with many awards and honorary degrees.

What Does *Gender and the Politics of History* Say?

According to *Gender and the Politics of History*, gender (the characteristics that serve to define what is considered "masculine" or "feminine") is not a biological fact. The definition of what is masculine and what is feminine changes according to when and where you look, Scott argues, because gender is a social construct.* That is, it is society that decides this definition, not nature. What is more, Scott says that gender is continually constructed to establish hierarchies. These hierarchies, she argues, are routinely unfavorable to women.

Scott begins her inquiry from a feminist perspective, considering the question of the persistence of inequality between men and women. If economic, political, and social inequality produce revolutions, she asks, how is it that we have lived with gender inequality for so long without any revolution?

Turning to theoretical models such as poststructuralism (an approach to culture and society often used to highlight the role of language and symbols in systems of power) and deconstruction* (a method of analysis often used for literary texts, in which concepts acquire their meaning through their relation to other words and concepts), Scott reaches a conclusion. The persistence of gender inequality owes a lot to the power of language to control and shape our understanding of gender itself.

Scott's work provided new theoretical tools to question forms of oppression justified by "natural" differences between females and males—differences in factors such as behavior, abilities, intellect, and disposition.

Gender and the Politics of History was highly influential. It made "gender" an important category of historical analysis, and it contributed significantly to a debate among historians on the aims and methods of the academic study of history. Indeed, its theoretical innovations (particularly the application of methods of analysis previously considered more appropriate to literature) have been taken up by scholars in many disciplines outside of history.

The work has been reprinted and translated into a number of languages, proving its continuing relevance. Even if a lot of its ideas are now the accepted view of many historians, as far as methods and aims are concerned, it continues to inspire emerging scholars to consider new ways of analyzing data and sources.

Scott's argument that gender is a socially constructed phenomenon continues to be relevant to newly opened fields such as queer theory.* This is an approach to cultural analysis that starts from the understanding that gender is neither innate nor stable. Both these arguments lie at the center of Scott's thesis.

Why Does *Gender and the Politics of History* Matter?

It is possible to argue that *Gender and the Politics of History* will continue to be important until scholars are no longer interested in inequalities between groups—inequalities that are justified on the grounds of natural and biological differences (between men and women, for example, or between people from different races).

The book's central argument about the socially constructed nature of gender, and the uses gender has been put to by systems of power arising from capitalism,* is a key strand of contemporary studies of history and society. It is difficult to obtain an accurate and comprehensive overview of the field of historical study today without some knowledge of this area. Indeed, issues of gender and language have become equally important throughout the humanities. Readings of contemporary art and literature require some knowledge of this strain of thought—as does contemporary politics at the national and global level.

Gender and the Politics of History provides an excellent theoretical introduction to an increasingly important feature of modern society: discussions and changes associated with gender and the use of language in continuing inequality. There is also much to be learned from the precision and clarity of Scott's analytical method. Using approaches that owe much to the theory of writers such as French philosopher Jacques Derrida* and cultural theorist Michel Foucault,* Scott's book provides an inspiring demonstration of the rigorous application of theory to cultural analysis.

SECTION 1
INFLUENCES

MODULE 1
THE AUTHOR AND THE
HISTORICAL CONTEXT

KEY POINTS

- Scott's book made gender an important category for historians and social theorists* conducting analysis in their fields.

- She gained her doctorate in the United States, at the University of Wisconsin-Madison—then a hotbed of left-wing student activism.

- When *Gender and the Politics of History* was published in 1988, there was a lot of interest in the academic world in French poststructuralist* theory, which challenged assumptions about knowledge and language.

Why Read This Text?

The nine essays by Joan Wallach Scott collected under the title *Gender and the Politics of History* represent a significant milestone in the academic study of history. At the time of publication in 1988, women's history was largely treated as a minority interest compared to major works of political, economic, and cultural history. Scott was interested in understanding why women remained on an unequal footing with men when the world had seen enormous economic, political, and social changes. She put forward a nuanced and subtle argument that understandings of gender had changed over time. In consequence, gender was a concept with a history of its own—a concept worthy of study.

Moreover, Scott argued that since gender describes sexual difference, studies of gender should not be read as studies of women

❝ My whole world was highly political. Political dividing lines were crucial for my parents and I saw the world that way, too. The formative lesson of those years for me was less an abiding Marxism than it was an abiding political mentality. ❞

Joan Wallach Scott, "An Interview with Joan Scott"

only. Terms such as "masculine" and "feminine" are contextual, she claimed; neither makes sense without the other. What is more, concepts of gender are created by social structures as a means of understanding sexual difference. And if gender exists in all eras and plays a significant role in social structure, then we cannot assume any understanding of gender to be universal.

According to Scott, gender should be a major subject of historical study in its own right, rather than simply existing alongside studies of economic, political, and cultural history. Her argument was aimed at historians of all stripes, and received attention from supporters and detractors alike. Her text is significant for the implications of its argument, for the challenge it lays down for those in the field of history, and for its lasting impact on the field of feminist* history.

Author's Life

Scott grew up in New York City where her parents were teachers and social activists, influenced by Marxism* and the political left. Her father was an active member of the Teachers Union in the 1950s and was forced to resign a position because of his Marxist politics. Scott has stated in interviews that this period of her life helped form her political views.

In 1962, Scott began a doctorate at the University of Wisconsin-Madison, then a hotbed of activism for the "New Left"*—a student movement campaigning for reform in areas such as gay rights, gender roles, and abortion.[1] She specialized in French history in graduate school and, influenced by the sociologist Charles Tilly,* her dissertation, which she finished in 1969, was a social history* of glassworkers in France during the late-nineteenth century. It did not reflect the interest in gender that would later be seen in *Gender and the Politics of History*.

Charles Tilly wrote about the structure of revolutions. We can perhaps detect his influence in Scott's *Gender and the Politics of History* if we consider the question that partially prompted her to write it. History has shown that economic, political, and social inequality produces revolutions. So why has gender inequality persisted for so long without revolution? Scott's answer is that this is due to the power of language to control and shape our understanding of gender itself.

Scott continued to work as a social historian for a decade at the University of Illinois, Northwestern University, and the University of North Carolina. In 1980, she joined Brown University in Providence, Rhode Island, where she became the founder-director of the Pembroke Center for Teaching and Research on Women. At Brown, she met feminist scholars in literary studies, many of them working in the field of French poststructuralism. Poststructuralist theory revolves around an understanding of culture and history that questions the existence of objective certainties and over-arching "structures" that are useful to the analysis of societies and literary texts.

French poststructuralist theory influenced both the research Scott published in the late 1980s and her later works. Several of the essays published in *Gender* first appeared in different peer-reviewed academic journals during this time. Through poststructuralist theory, Scott explained, she could now deal with questions such as the persistence of gender inequalities despite massive social change.

Author's Background

Scott had been working as a historian since the late 1960s. Like most of her peers she was influenced by 1960s counterculture* and the

Civil Rights Movement,* and later by second-wave feminism.* This was a more political and social strand of feminism that followed "first-wave feminism," in which women had demanded the vote and equal recognition under the law.

Scott wrote several notable essays during a political revival of conservative values in the United States signaled by the election of a right-wing Republican* president, Ronald Reagan,* in 1980. Left-leaning scholars like Scott saw this political turn as an assault on the move toward social equality of the previous two decades.

Feminists, in particular, considered the ideologies and theories that had sustained the social movements of the 1960s to be insufficient or ineffective in light of new, conservative circumstances. The liberalizing* policies of the Soviet Union in the late 1980s—the "thaw" in the oppressive communist* political environment—and the dominance of conservative political parties in the United States and the United Kingdom shaped the political context of the decade. In response, historians began to revise the aims and methods of Marxist, social, and women's history.

NOTES

1   Elaine Abelson et al., "Interview with Joan Scott," *Radical History Review* 45 (1989): 42.

MODULE 2
ACADEMIC CONTEXT

KEY POINTS

- The major concern of gender studies is to understand how gender differences are used as a method of domination.

- In the 1980s, gender history was increasingly drawing from the works of French literary and cultural theorists associated with poststructuralist* thought.

- Scott adopted the ideas of the French cultural theorist Michel Foucault* to explain how gender acts as a category of power and domination.

The Work in its Context

Joan Wallach Scott's *Gender and the Politics of History* examines how gender is used as a means to develop social stratification—the division of society along lines of wealth and social status—and to construct systems of dominance.

Scott argues that gender does not arise from experience or nature. Instead it is created for the purpose of establishing the political and economic power of men and subordinating women. As Scott puts it, "gender is a primary way of signifying relations of power."[1] At the time Scott wrote *Gender*, scholars were preoccupied with power,[2] then understood to be the process of exerting domination over others.

Scott builds her critique on an analysis of the nature of knowledge. As she writes in *Gender*, the prevailing notion is that knowledge closely mirrors experience. According to this view, if a historian wants to understand the past, it is enough to simply describe it. But Scott's conclusion is different. Knowledge, she argues, is the product of the ways in which languages and symbols represent experience. It is not

> ❝ If gender could be argued to be a key field of experience for both men and women—for *all* people—then one might posit gender as a subject of universal relevance. This was the political context for Joan Wallach Scott's splendid essay 'Gender: A Useful Category of Historical Analysis,' which opened the December 1986 issue of the *American Historical Review*, a commanding placement in a flagship journal of the profession. ❞
>
> Jeanne Boydston, "Gender as a Question of Historical Analysis"

simply the product of experience itself. Scott suggests that if a historian wants to analyze and critique the ways in which notions such as gender have changed over time, first he or she will have to reject experience as the basis of all knowledge.

She turned to French literary theory to find a new understanding of the nature of knowledge. Poststructuralism—an approach to culture that has been used to highlight the role of language and symbol in systems of power—offered Scott a method of analyzing the ways in which society creates knowledge about gender. From here she began a study of the ways in which knowledge has changed over time. The object of her analysis, of course, was the historical creation of gender.

In the early 1980s, when Scott wrote the essays collected in *Gender and the Politics of History*, the intellectual environment was in flux, particularly in academic circles in the United States. She thought that history, and notably women's history, had not shown a great deal of theoretical development in the previous decades and tended to be overly descriptive. The text's intended audience, then, was scholars researching social history* and women's history, particularly those dealing with modern and contemporary periods in Europe and the US.

Using literary theory that owed a debt to poststructuralism and the work of the French cultural-theorist Michel Foucault, Scott aimed to intervene in women's history and, more broadly, in social history. She proposed that gender is a concept created by society, and—contrary to the assumptions of much history written at the time—it does not describe a permanent, stable reality.[3]

Overview of the Field

Scott's approach to writing history changed when she was a professor at Brown University. During the late 1970s and early 1980s, she became part of a community of feminist* literary scholars who, going against the dominant ideology of contemporary English-language historians, were translating and using the works of French theorists to advance their field.[4] Scott started using theory to formulate a concept of gender and to critique social history.

Scott's work was timely. It represented one of the two key ways in which women's history was approached: as a history of the victimized, or as a history of how societies create victims. The work of the feminist historian Linda Gordon* perhaps exemplifies the first type of history and Scott's work, the second.

Similarly, the scholar Mary Poovey* appears to share Scott's perspective in her book *Uneven Developments: The Ideological Work of Gender in Mid-Victorian England* (1988). Here, like Scott, Poovey argues that gender is socially constructed and used to establish a social hierarchy that favors men. The work of the scholar Diana Fuss,* on the other hand, takes an intermediate position, attempting to combine aspects of the two perspectives.

Scott's articles about gender appeared at a time when research into women's history and the work of feminist historians were increasingly dismissed from larger historical discussions about politics and economics. Some academics also regarded the field of women's history as a redundant area in which to specialize. In this context Scott tried to use gender as an analytical category, with the aim of expanding feminist influence. She defined the history of gender as the history of sexual difference. Studying gender did not mean simply studying women, it meant studying how the meaning of sexual differences was established and the ways in which it served society.

Scott wanted to use gender to analyze a broader set of topics than would have been allowed by the history of women. Among these were war, foreign relations, and other subjects not usually analyzed from a gender perspective. Wanting to use gender history to change our understanding of the past, Scott argued that for too long women's history had simply worked alongside the accepted historical narratives of political and economic change without challenging it.

Academic Influences

Gender and the Politics of History is set apart from other works of social history by the extent to which it was influenced by French theory, by feminist scholars, and by social historians such as E. P. Thompson.* Inspired by a wide range of thinkers, including the cultural critic Michel Foucault, the theorist Judith Butler,* the sociologist Charles Tilly,* and the English literature scholar Diana Fuss, Scott's work lays out a new agenda for feminist historians.

Scott is one of a generation of academics who explicitly state that generating knowledge through research is not a neutral process and cannot escape a political agenda or context.[5] Indeed, Scott's own agenda is clear. As a feminist she looks to analyze and then appraise forms of social organization where domination—political or economic—is achieved or justified in the name of biological or "natural" differences.

A key term for her project, as the work's title makes clear, is "gender." According to Scott herself, the definition of gender, as it is commonly used today, originated within the political and intellectual arena known as "second-wave feminism."* Scott began her career as a scholar in the 1970s as second-wave feminism came to prominence. With it came the argument that biology and instincts did not necessarily determine the relations between human beings. In other words, social roles were not defined by "nature."

Although the book's key ideas are original to the author, they build upon a work that she co-authored with the sociologist Louise Tilly*: *Women, Work, and Family*.[6] In it, Scott and Tilly describe the diversity of women's experiences as laborers in industrial society. They resist generalizations so as not to create a universalized conception of "woman." Scott carries this idea forward in *Gender*.

To arrive at the argument of *Gender and the Politics of History*, Scott built on an on-going intellectual inquiry into the relationship between language and reality. In particular, Scott relied on theorists who argued that language does not relate directly to reality, and what we know comes more from language than it does from our experience of reality—perhaps entirely so.

NOTES

1   Joan Wallach Scott, "Gender: A Useful Category of Historical Analysis," *American Historical Review* 91 (1986): 1067.

2   Jeanne Boydston, "Gender as a Question of Historical Analysis," *Gender & History* 20 (2008): 563.

3   Diana Fuss's *Essentially Speaking: Feminism, Nature and Difference* (New York: Routledge, 1989) offers a useful critique of analyzing gender as either essence or social construct.

4   Sue Morgan, "Theorizing Feminist History: A Thirty-Year Retrospective," *Women's History Review* 18 (2009): 385.

5   Morgan, "Theorizing Feminist History," 385.

6   Louise A. Tilly and Joan Wallach Scott, *Women, Work, and Family* (New York: Holt, Reinhart and Winston, 1978).

MODULE 3
THE PROBLEM

KEY POINTS

- *Gender and the Politics of History* attempted to look at the way social and political life had been constructed to see how this might have reinforced the idea of inequality between men and women.

- When *Gender* was first published in 1988 women's history was primarily focused on uncovering and recovering the actions of women from the past.

- Many social historians* at the time were concerned that the way Scott was looking at gender issues led to difficult questions about long-held ways of looking at reality.

Core Question

The core question Joan Wallach Scott was looking to answer in *Gender and the Politics of History* was how differences, particularly those differences between humans classified as female or male, have been constructed throughout history. In other words: Scott analyzed the uses, creations, implementations, justifications, and transformations of these differences in social and political life in order to explain the persistence of inequality between women and men.

The question was important for both theoretical and political reasons. First, it was a contribution to the analysis of power, one of the fundamental questions of the social sciences. Second, for both feminist* historians and for the wider feminist movement alike, Scott's work provided new theoretical tools to question forms of oppression justified by "natural" differences between females and males— differences in factors such as behavior, abilities, intellect, and disposition.

> **"** 'Gender' does not carry with it a necessary statement about inequality or power nor does it name the aggrieved (and hitherto invisible) party. Whereas the term 'women's history' proclaims its politics by asserting (contrary to customary practice) that women are valid historical subjects, 'gender' includes but does not name women and seems to pose no critical threat. **"**
> Joan Wallach Scott, "Gender: A Useful Category of Historical Analysis"

To arrive at her idea of gender history, Scott adapted the theories of other authors, notably the French poststructuralist* writers and the cultural theorist Michel Foucault.* Feminist scholars like Judith Butler,* Denise Riley,* and Carolyn Walker Bynum* also influenced her work.

Scott turned these intellectual resources to the project of rewriting feminist history through an investigation of the ways in which sex differences between men and women were not natural, but were artificially constructed—and how these differences served to structure and legitimize relationships built on unequal power.

The Participants

Scott's *Gender and the Politics of History* offered a challenge to the field of women's history. Until this point, most women's history was descriptive, and was primarily involved in the recovery of things that prominent women had done in the past that had been neglected by previous historical research.

Historians of women helped identify new facts about the past in order to understand them. But, for the most part, theoretical considerations were left aside. As Scott wrote: "The proliferation of case studies in women's history seems to call for some synthesizing perspective ... [T]he discrepancy between the high quality of recent work in women's history and the continuing marginal status of the field as a whole ... points up the limits of descriptive approaches that do not address dominant disciplinary concepts ... in terms that can shake their power and perhaps transform them."[1]

She also criticized social history. For her, social history assumed that "gender difference [could] be explained within its existing frame of [economic] explanation" and that gender was "not an issue requiring study in itself."[2]

Similarly, Scott questioned the methods of certain social historians and the Marxist* assumptions behind them. For her, the Marxist premise that gender issues were only interesting in as far as they resulted from other issues, such as economics and production, was not enough.

The Contemporary Debate

Considering the contemporary debate, it is worthwhile noting that Scott rejected the view that feminism should adopt an essential definition of "woman." She argued instead that "woman" was a changeable concept, and feminists should examine how societies have continually re-invented it.

In the book's last section Scott considers the dilemmas of two opposed feminist political strategies: *equality* and *difference*. She explains that feminists who argue that sexual difference is an irrelevant concern in social realms such as employment favor the strategy of equality. Feminists who advocate for women's rights in terms of the characteristics women share as a group, favor the strategy of difference.[3]

Scott argues that by defining women according to their shared characteristics or experiences, scholars are creating a universal, essentialized version of women. By doing so, it is easy to lose sight both of society's role in constructing the concept of gender and of how that concept is used to oppress or victimize.

Although this debate was central to the study of women's history at the time, Scott stood apart from other scholars by drawing on theorists such as Michel Foucault and from poststructuralist methods like deconstruction.* This is a method of literary analysis founded on the assumption that the meaning of any concept—gender, for example—has no self-evident meaning or value, because it is dependent on other concepts. Many social historians disliked some of the philosophical premises of poststructuralism. For them, it questioned the possibility of knowing and explaining material reality. Scott, however, found that it offered possibilities.

Foucault's explanations of how society's powerful members create knowledge, meanwhile, provided the foundation on which Scott built her argument that gender is a concept created by society for the sake of establishing hierarchy.

NOTES

1   Joan Wallach Scott, "Gender: A Useful Category of Historical Analysis," *American Historical Review* 91 (1986): 1055.

2   Joan Wallach Scott, *Gender and the Politics of History* (New York: Columbia University Press, 1999), 22.

3   Scott, *Gender and the Politics of History*, 167–9.

MODULE 4
THE AUTHOR'S CONTRIBUTION

KEY POINTS

- Scott wanted to show that the construction of gender differences was central to capitalist* social organization.
- *Gender and the Politics of History* made "gender" a central category of analysis for historians.
- The work was influenced by the writings of French poststructuralists.*

Author's Aims

Joan Wallach Scott's main aims in writing *Gender and the Politics of History* were to innovate in the field of women's history, and to find new ways to make the topics feminists* were thinking about and were interested in theoretically and politically relevant.

Scott was a social historian,* influenced by the politics of the American left. Her empirical work dealt with labor,* labor organization, industrialization* (the period of social and economic change characterized by the rise of large-scale means of production), and capitalism* (the economic system in which the means of production are concentrated largely or entirely in private hands). In addition to introducing a novel method of analysis, she wanted to explain how gender differences were a central part of capitalism's organization.

In contrast to social historians such as the British Marxist* scholar E. P. Thompson,* Scott thought that the subordinate position of women in capitalist societies was not simply a condition that had been inherited from the domestic set-ups that had existed previously. For her, even the modern division of labor*—at least in countries in the

❝ To find gender in history … it is not enough to do the literal, thematic reading typical of the discipline; a different kind of exegesis is required. Here the work of literary critics associated with poststructuralism has been extremely helpful for me. They point to the importance of textuality, to the ways arguments are structured and presented as well as to what is literally said. ❞

Joan Wallach Scott, *Gender and the Politics of History*

West during the nineteenth and twentieth centuries—was again based around gender and was divided into gender-specific roles in words like "household" and "workplace." For her, these distinctions belonged to, and therefore helped to define, capitalist societies.

By its method, then, Scott's work is connected to theoretical ideas about how language controls and shapes our knowledge and experience of gender. By its subject, it is connected to feminist and women's history. By its way of analyzing, it is connected to Marxist thought.

Scott does not, however, adhere strictly to the expectations of any of these connections. In particular, she extends the ideas of Marxism, which focuses on matters of economics and labor, to examine the role gender plays in shaping society. When it comes to feminism, she rejects the idea that women are essentially the same in their experience of gender, and that societies create gender definitions that reflect broader values and social desires.

Approach

Scott developed her ideas as a critique both of scholarly uses of the concept of gender and the theoretical underpinnings of contemporary social history.

Since the 1970s, feminist scholars had increasingly understood gender to be a social construct* of sexual difference rather than a biological fact.[1] Scott was original, however, in her use of deconstruction,* a method of cultural analysis developed by the French philosopher Jacques Derrida,* according to which we cannot depend on any term or concept to have a stable, dependable meaning rooted in a material reality. She turned to deconstructionism first to analyze the formation of meanings of gender, and then to investigate broader historical matters.

For her, the goal is to examine gender "concretely and in context and to consider it a historical phenomenon, produced, reproduced and transformed in different situations over time."[2] But to do this, historians first must question the reliability of terms that have been previously taken as self-evident. For Scott, history is not "about the things that happened to women and men and how they reacted to them" but "about how the subjective and collective meanings of women and men as categories of identity have been constructed."[3]

Scott insists that restricting gender and sex analysis to the realm of the family and using categories such as class to analyze all other social relations is limiting. She argues that it is important for historians to analyze gender because gender is "an aspect of social organization generally." For her, "sexual difference is invoked and contested as many kinds of struggles of power."[4]

Contribution in Context

Scott arrived at her main concept partly by reading the works of writers associated with poststructuralism like Jacques Derrida and Michel Foucault,* and by interacting with feminist literary scholars such as Judith Butler.*

The persistence of inequality that is justified on the basis of "natural" difference is a question she returns to throughout her work. And although she had previously produced material on women and history, the methods she used to address it changed in the 1980s—notably in *Gender and the Politics of History*.

Gender reflected the growing interest in interpreting women's history as the history of oppression or—as Scott emphasized—as the history of how society has constructed inequality. This is a perspective Scott gained from Foucault. For him there was no history of inequality. It was a question of how inequality was created by society.[5] The two methods of approaching women's history—as the history of the victims of inequality or as the history of society's creation of inequality—encapsulates the framework of Scott's work.[6]

NOTES

1   Sue Morgan, "Theorising Feminist History: a Thirty-Year Retrospective," *Women's History Review* 18, no. 3 (2009): 381–407.

2   Joan Wallach Scott, *Gender and the Politics of History* (New York: Columbia University Press, 1999), 6.

3   Scott, *Gender and the Politics of History*, 6.

4   Scott, *Gender and the Politics of History*, 6.

5   Selya Benhabib, *Situating the Self: Gender, Community and Postmodernism in Contemporary Ethics* (New York: Routledge, 1992), 222.

6   This framework is evident in the debate between Scott and Linda Gordon, and in the work of Diana Fuss. See Joan Wallach Scott, "Response to Review on *Gender and the Politics of History*," *Signs* 15(4), 859–60 and Linda Gordon, "Response to Scott," *Signs* 15(4), 852–3; Diana Fuss, *Essentially Speaking: Feminism, Nature and Difference* (New York: Routledge, 1989).

SECTION 2
IDEAS

MODULE 5
MAIN IDEAS

KEY POINTS

- The key theme of Scott's book is the social and linguistic construction of gender differences.
- Scott argues that gender is a useful category for historical and political analysis.
- Social historians* opposed Scott's argument that, fundamentally, reality was constructed around language.

Key Themes

At the heart of Joan Wallach Scott's *Gender and the Politics of History* is the argument that gender differences are constructed linguistically and socially—through language and society. This theme emerges from Scott's definition of gender as "a constitutive element of social relationships based on perceived differences between the sexes [and] a primary way of signifying relationships of power."[1]

The opposition between male and female appears, she argues, through five modes of organization:

- Cultural symbols
- Normative concepts—rules that define correct, proper or normal ways of behavior
- Power relations—relationships that establish hierarchies between different individuals and social groups
- Politics
- Subjectivity—the process through which an individual constructs a sense of their private self-identity

❝ When one rereads *The Making of the English Working Class* now, one is struck not by the absence of women in the narrative but by the awkward way in which they figure there. The book illuminates some of the reasons for the difficulty and frustration experienced by contemporary feminist* socialists as they tried to convince themselves and their colleagues that there ought to be a place for women in the narrative of class formation and in the theory of politics that narrative contains. **❞**

Joan Wallach Scott, *Gender and the Politics of History*

For Scott, there are two main tasks for historians of gender:
- To analyze the changes, continuities, and the specific content of these five modes in different time periods
- To analyze the relationships among these modes

Her book is structured to make the case that gender is a basic element in relations of power and that "sexual difference is a primary way of signifying differentiation"[2] and forming meaning in politics. This requires Scott to consider how gender differences are produced. And she shows that class, the economic and labor* market, and equality before the law can be gendered.

Scott rejects the assumption that words have a fixed meaning. For her, a word has no "sense," strictly speaking, without an understanding of its difference from other words. So "woman" or "female" gain their meaning through their opposition to "man" and "masculine."

Exploring the Ideas

Gender and the Politics of History is a collection of essays that collectively seek to develop the concept of gender as a useful category of historical and political analysis.

The first three essays are theoretical. Here, Scott thoroughly explains her definition of gender. Then she investigates two works on British labor history, first analyzing *Languages of Class* (1983) by the historian Gareth Stedman Jones* before reassessing the evidence used by E. P. Thompson* in his classic historical work *The Making of the English Working Class* (1963).

Scott argues that social historians had struggled to offer accounts of women as significant contributors to historical events, and as fundamental to discussions of how social classes were formed. In seminal works of 1960s social history, she claims, "the organization of the story and the master codes that structure the narrative are gendered in such a way as to confirm rather than challenge the masculine representation of class."[3]

In the next three essays, Scott applies the method of linguistic analysis known as deconstruction* and French thinker Michel Foucault's* theory of power to the concept of gender, using case studies. In these chapters, she analyzes the organization and activism of the Parisian Garment Trades in the revolutions of 1848,* the Parisian Industrial Statistical Survey of 1847–8, and the writings of nineteenth-century French political economists.

In the final two chapters, she first analyzes how understandings of gender were expressed in, and how they influenced, a lawsuit about labor discrimination at the American department store Sears.* Then she investigates the organization of the American Historical Association* as an institution, in practices of exclusion and marginalization.

An additional chapter, a critical review of the uses of gender as a concept, was added in the revised edition of 1999. This section reiterates that gender and politics are interdependent systems.

Language and Expression

During the 1980s, the "intellectual battlefield" of social and labor history was concerned with methods of research and analysis—

particularly the ways in which any method actually shaped the study. Social historians saw themselves as materialists,* who observed reality and offered analyses of the past. They criticized Scott for promoting a theory that preferred the analysis of language to the analysis of material reality.

Since she used a method developed in literary studies, other social historians, among them William Sewell* and Bryan Palmer,* accused her of focusing exclusively on texts. For them, documenting people's real experiences was a more worthwhile endeavor. Palmer insisted that Scott and other poststructuralists* neglected the material world in favor of language and representation.[4]

In part, Scott's fiercest critics were echoing a wider dispute about the value of literary theory in the discipline of academic history. Understanding this dispute will assist in a better reading of Scott's work.

In response to criticism of her method, Scott acknowledges that the historian primarily observes and reports on material reality. But to do so, he or she must also understand the ways in which language— the language of gender, for example—shapes and even controls the meaning of what is being observed.

Scott's work is based on questioning fixed meanings. She is suspicious of any position that claims neutrality, objectivity, or universality, and specifically questions universal claims about class or gender.

NOTES

1   Joan Wallach Scott, *Gender and the Politics of History* (New York: Columbia University Press, 1999), 42.

2   Scott, *Gender and the Politics of History*, 45.

3   Scott, *Gender and the Politics of History*, 72.

4   Bryan D. Palmer, "Critical Theory, Historical Materialism, and the Ostensible End of Marxism: The Poverty of Theory Revisited," *International Review of Social History* 38 (1993): 151–2.

MODULE 6
SECONDARY IDEAS

KEY POINTS

- Scott's *Gender and the Politics of History* challenged the way that social historians* had used and defined the concept of class.

- Scott argues that concepts like class and gender have changed over time. They have their own history.

- Ongoing debates about feminism* as a potential tool of imperialism*—that is, "empire building"—also owe a debt to Scott.

Other Ideas

An important secondary strand of Joan Wallach Scott's *Gender and the Politics of History* is her assessment of the ways in which social historians approach the issue of class.[1] She focuses on the work of the Marxist* historian E. P. Thompson* and his influential book *The Making of the English Working Class* (1963).

In Thompson's framework, the experience of subordinate social groups was determined by their own actions. It was not the result of existing structures or the interests of dominant groups. For Scott, this definition obscured the process that constituted class itself. It also presented social and economic relations, or the way that people relate to each other socially and economically, as pre-existing structures that appeared to be independent of politics.

For Scott, class is a linguistic construction rather than an objective condition reflecting existing methods of economic organization and production. In her analysis, "worker" has no meaning unless opposed to the word "boss," while categories such as "workers" or "citizens"

❝ Scott strongly criticizes all cultural and political ideas that assume unchanging differences or fixed oppositions, including the belief in an 'essential' French universalism that opposes an 'essential' Islamic particularism. ❞

Lloyd Kramer, "The Politics of the Veil by Joan Wallach Scott"

rely on previously established gender polarities—routinely "male" at one end and "female" at the other—to structure their meaning.

In *Gender and the Politics of History*, Scott examines how the concept of class and productive work have been constructed throughout history. To do this, she uses sources about workers in nineteenth-century France. Her key idea, that society creates these structures and that they are neither pre-existing nor universal, is to be understood as having developed in resistance to views like Thompson's.

Exploring the Ideas

To understand Scott's appraisals of class and gender, it is useful to have some background knowledge of the historiography* of British social history—that is, the ways in which British social history has been approached in writing.

Much of Scott's work takes the form of a theoretical examination of the profession of academic history. Throughout her book, her aim is to show that gender is a useful category for historical analysis. But she argues, too, that the meaning of social categories such as gender and class are not stable and that they change over time. The categories themselves, in other words, have a history—and historians who do not recognize that these changes occur in response to uses of political power run the risk of furthering inequality and oppression in society. Consequently her work extends a moral challenge to historians.

Scott asks how categories of class were formulated at specific historical moments, and how one definition emerged as the dominant one. Historians of labor* and gender working in different geographical areas and time periods took up this task.[2]

Scott believes the real-world applications of these ideas are political. Her work asks, for example, who uses the term "class" and for what ends. Cultural and social movements can incorporate Scott's critical discussion of categories such as class and gender to intervene in the public sphere and promote equality in societies.

Overlooked

An overlooked argument made in *Gender and the Politics of History* concerns the issue of whether feminist strategy should be founded on assumptions of equality or difference—an important debate in feminist theory and politics. For the author, difference and equality are not opposites (she insists that, since "power is constructed on difference,"[3] power must also be challenged). What is more, "equality" should not be defined as "sameness."

Returning to these topics in her recent book *The Politics of the Veil*, about Muslim presence in political and cultural life in twentieth- and twenty-first-century France, Scott examines French law on secularity and conspicuous religious symbols passed in 2004 that particularly targeted the headscarf worn by Muslim women, and France's resistance to social, cultural, and religious differences.[4] She argues that the French ideology* of abstract universalism,* is based on an understanding of citizenship that has been put together from a male perspective. It is assumed to be "universal," and applying to all. But those who defined what universalism is are in fact trying to obtain a better understanding of themselves. In other words, French universalism is an expression of the desire of the dominant section of French society to find an answer to some kind of psychological predicament.

Scott considers this desire to be impossible to resolve. And the real result of trying to attempt this through universalism is an intolerance of what people from the dominant section of French society might perceive as "other."

It is useful to reconsider this aspect of Scott's book in the light of current debate about "feminism as imperialism." This debate began after the attacks of September 11, 2001* in the United States, when the problem of the oppression of women in countries such as Afghanistan was used to justify military intervention. The Turkish political scientist Deniz Kandiyoti* has contributed to this discussion by proposing, for example, that we should avoid "the facile dualities of Western impositions versus indigenous culture"[5] if we are to usefully discuss the meaning of women's rights in Afghanistan.

In a sense, this type of reasoning echoes Scott's ideas about questioning concepts and assumptions that reduce ideas to overly simple essential opposites such as "Western values" and "non-Western values."

NOTES

1 Joan Wallach Scott, *Gender and the Politics of History* (New York: Columbia University Press, 1999), ch. 4.

2 For example, Gail Hershatter and Wang Zheng, "Chinese History: A Useful Category of Gender Analysis," *The American Historical Review* 113, no. 5 (2008): 1404–21.

3 Joan Wallach Scott, "Deconstructing Equality-Versus-Difference: Or, the Uses of Poststructuralist Theory for Feminism" in *The Postmodern Turn: New Perspectives on Social Theory*, ed. Steve Seidman (Cambridge University Press, 1994), 298.

4 Joan Wallach Scott, *The Politics of the Veil* (Princeton, NJ: Princeton University Press, 2007).

5 Deniz Kandiyoti, *The Politics of Gender and Reconstruction in Afghanistan* (Geneva: UNRISD, 2005), 3.

MODULE 7
ACHIEVEMENT

KEY POINTS

- Scott made gender an important category of historical analysis.

- *Gender and the Politics of History* was published at a time in which a "linguistic turn"* was taking place in the discipline of history.

- Scott's book has been criticized for being centered on European concerns and history.

Assessing the Argument

In *Gender and the Politics of History* Joan Wallach Scott posed the following question: if historians have shown that economic, political, and social inequality produces revolutions, then why have they been unable to show why gender inequality has persisted for so long without revolutionary change?

Scott's answer links her work to many of her contemporaries. Due to the power and ability of language to control and shape our understanding of gender (and experience more generally), inequality has continued almost unnoticed by historians. By placing language under special scrutiny, Scott links her work to thinkers such as Jacques Derrida,* who described how the meaning of words does not depend on reality but, rather, on the meaning of other words.

Focusing on the ways in which language shapes our understanding of history, Scott played an important part in what is often called "the linguistic turn." Her interest in important issues in society such as gender oppression, class struggle, and revolution saw her associated

❝Joan Scott's 1988 book *Gender and the Politics of History* was important in helping to bridge real divides and to inspire the virtual explosion in feminist histories of Latin America published in the last twenty years.**❞**
Heidi Tinsman, "A Paradigm of Our Own"

with sociologists, such as Charles Tilly,* who study the history of large-scale social changes.

These interests also connected Scott to Marxist*-influenced scholars, who were interested in her work for its ability to identify and locate a basic struggle in society, that of gender.

Achievement in Context

Gender and the Politics of History had an immediate impact on many different disciplines and has remained relevant since its publication in 1988. Scott is now considered one of the scholars who changed historical practice during a shift that took place since the late 1970s— what is known as the "linguistic turn."

As academic thinking about the role language plays in the construction of reality remains relevant, so too does Scott's work. Scholars continue to draw on her use of gender as a tool in historical analysis as they research ways in which political power is structured in society. *Gender* can therefore be considered a foundational text in contemporary women's history and feminist* scholarship.

Since *Gender's* publication, historians of different regions and periods have been using gender as a category of historical analysis, just as Scott suggested they should. They have used aspects of Scott's idea and then conducted research through the lens of gender, as a category that develops and changes.[1]

Scott's suggestions about the importance of language, of a society's symbols, of the concepts that shape what is "normal" and acceptable in society, and of the role of politics and social institutions in the study of gender history, all helped mark an important conceptual turn. For scholars of contemporary capitalism,* a "focus on gender and sexuality helped to establish the historical and historiographical* significance of feminized consumption alongside masculinized production."[2]

The concept of gender as a category of analysis has now been adapted and used to expand the discussion on a growing number of topics. For example, Scott has been influential for historians of Latin America working on the history of the region's states. Scholars researching subjects like indigenous communities and peasants during the period of Spanish rule used Scott's work to redefine the concept of patriarchy.* The term is now used as a gendered category of analysis "not as an overarching 'system' or result of 'nature,' but as a heterogeneous and contradictory set of dynamics and meanings: symbols, institutional arrangements, normative pacts, subjective identities."[3]

Limitations

In her book, Scott argues that gender is a central field of experience for all people since it is "a primary way of signifying relations of power."[4] Nonetheless, scholars such as the American historian Jeanne Boydston* have pointed out that Scott's conception of power, based on the work of Michel Foucault,* is a modern Western concept that might not be applicable outside the West.

According to Foucault, power is a "process of creating advantage— the 'differential control over or access to material and symbolic resources'—with the goal of exercising dominion."[5] But, for Boydston, power also operates through "socially dispersed forms of interiorized self-discipline that are fundamentally western European and bourgeois."[6] So, for those cultures not defined by an oppositional binary between male and female, perceived differences between the bodies of males and females do not form part of a construction of domination (as it is understood in Foucault's terms). Readers of different cultural backgrounds, then, have interpreted the ideas of the text differently.

The Nigerian historian Oyeronke Oyewumi* has explained that "Western gender categories are presented as inherent in nature (of bodies) and operate on a dichotomous, binarily opposed male/female, man/woman duality in which the male is assumed to be superior and therefore the defining category." This, she says, is "particularly alien to many African cultures."[7]

Historians of Native American cultures such as Will Roscoe* and Jeanne Boydston have insisted that scholars look for other categories beyond masculinity and femininity, to indigenous conceptions of the body and the spirit world, for example.[8]

Another critic is the Iranian scholar Afsaneh Najmabadi,* who asks if gender and sexuality are useful categories beyond the modern historical period. In her own work, Najmabadi discovered the importance of age in considerations of gender.[9] Categories of modern sexuality that use the male–female binary* as a template did not work for Najmabadi's analysis of nineteenth-century Iranian culture. Concepts of sexual attractiveness in Qajar Iran (which existed from 1794 to 1925) did not differentiate between the sexes. She argues that the male–female binary was only required and adopted by the formation of the modern state.[10]

NOTES

1   Judith Surkis, "When Was the Linguistic Turn? A Genealogy," *The American Historical Review* 117, no. 3 (2012): 720.

2   Surkis, "When Was the Linguistic Turn?": 720.

3   Heidi Tinsman, "A Paradigm of Our Own: Joan Scott in Latin American History," *The American Historical Review* 113, no. 5 (2008): 1368.

4   Joan Wallach Scott, *Gender and the Politics of History* (New York: Columbia University Press, 1999), 44.

5   For a critical examination of Foucault's theories and colonialism see Ann Laura Stoler, *Race and the Education of Desire: Foucault's History of Sexuality and the Colonial Order of Things* (Durham: Duke University Press, 1995).

6   Jeanne Boydston, "Gender as a Question of Historical Analysis," *Gender & History* 20 (2008): 573.

7   Oyeronke Oyewumi, "Conceptualizing Gender: The Eurocentric Foundations of Feminist Concepts and the Challenge of African Epistemologies," *Jenda: a Journal of Culture and African Woman Studies* 2(2002): 4.

8   Boydston, "Gender as a Question of Historical Analysis," 573.

9   Afsaneh Najmabadi, "Beyond the Americas," *Journal of Women's History* 18, no. 1 (2006): 12.

10 Afsaneh Najmabadi, "Mapping Transformations of Sex, Gender, and Sexuality in Modern Iran," *Social Analysis* 49, no. 2 (2005); Najmabadi, "Beyond the Americas."

PLACE IN THE AUTHOR'S WORK

KEY POINTS

- *Gender and the Politics of History* gave wide exposure to the methodological and theoretical contributions Scott had made to the field of women's history in the 1970s and 1980s.

- Scot has applied and developed the methods she used in *Gender* to her other works.

- The book's analysis of the ways in which social hierarchies are founded on the language of gender has been very influential the field of women's history.

Positioning

Joan Wallach Scott's *Gender and the Politics of History* is a collection of nine essays, many of which had previously been published. The first version of several of these essays appeared in different peer-reviewed academic journals during the 1980s while Scott was the founder-director of the Pembroke Center for Teaching and Research on Women at Brown University in the United States. Scott headed the inaugural research program, "Cultural Constructions of the Female," funded by the Ford Foundation and the National Endowment for the Humanities. The book builds on an earlier work: *Women, Work, and Family* (1978),[1] co-authored with Louise Tilly,* in which the diverse nature of women's experiences as laborers in industrial society is described. It is worth noting again that Scott and Tilly reject the idea that there is a universal conception of "woman," and are resistant to drawing general conclusions from the experiences they describe in their research.

66 Poststructuralist theory incorporated ideas such as the decentering of the subject and the abandonment of 'grand narratives,' but is probably best known for its affirmation of the centrality of language in the creation of (historical) meaning. The work of ... Joan Scott ... quickly became synonymous with this approach as [she] reconceptualized existing readings of gender by focusing not on the comparative historical experiences of women and men but on the way in which gender discourse operated as 'a primary way of signifying relationships of power.' 99

Sue Morgan, "Theorising Feminist History: A Thirty-Year Retrospective"

At the time that *Gender and the Politics of History* was published, Scott was already a recognized professor in the field of French social history* and women's history. The book proved important because it gave wider exposure to the methodological and theoretical issues she had developed over the previous two decades.

Integration

Scott developed a method of analyzing how conceptions of gender have changed over time. She became an important figure in an academic movement sometimes described as the "linguistic turn"* or "cultural history."* In subsequent works, Scott applied the methods she developed in *Gender* to historical case studies. In a work entitled *Only Paradoxes to Offer: French Feminists* and the Rights of Man* (1996), she analyzed how French feminists have taken the dominant political systems of the eighteenth, nineteenth, and twentieth centuries and put them to their own uses. In more recent works, she has applied her methodology to produce political appraisals of contemporary societies.

Scott's text *Parité! Sexual Equality and the Crisis of French Universalism* (2005), for instance, critically examined efforts in France to establish political equality between men and women.[2] The outcome, she argued, was an "essentialized" (that is, falsely universal) definition of gender that did not offer an explanation of the role society played in its creation.

In her *The Politics of the Veil* (2007), Scott turned to twenty-first century French politics and applied her analysis of gender difference to build her critique of the French national ban on headscarves.[3]

Significance

Gender and the Politics of History is one of Scott's better known and most influential works. The book has had a substantial impact on subsequent scholarship in various disciplines. Since its publication, historical case studies of women's activities in different time periods have been less descriptive and, in some cases, have even been replaced with works about the way gendered language has been used to construct social hierarchies. The study of how gender—in interaction with other analytical categories like "class" and "race"—constitutes power relationships is now commonplace in academic departments in many Western universities. This is in part due to Scott's success. She popularized techniques of inquiry that use the theories of the French thinker Michel Foucault,* as well as other work related to poststructuralist* thought, now typically associated with the linguistic turn—the academic current that turned to theories of language to solve certain issues of knowledge.

Scott's understanding of gender as the cultural meanings that become attached to sexual difference, and also as something that has shaped our understanding of history, has influenced the wider debate on gender and society. In her work, she has persuasively demonstrated the many ways in which gender plays a crucial role in the power relations that lie behind and continually color social practices and political discussions. She has contributed to the understanding that gender works as a set of fundamental assumptions that affect power relations within society.

Scott's work, then, allows for gender to become a proper analytic category for research in areas not conventionally considered the territory of women, or in which women do not feature explicitly as the key social or political drivers. Her method and arguments remind us of anthropology and also of the strand of cultural and linguistic analysis known as "critical theory."*

NOTES

1   Louise A. Tilly and Joan Wallach Scott, *Women, Work, and Family* (New York: Holt, Reinhart and Winston, 1978).

2   Joan Wallach Scott, *Parité! Sexual Equality and the Crisis of French Universalism* (Chicago: University of Chicago Press, 2005).

3   Joan Wallach Scott, *The Politics of the Veil* (Princeton, NJ: Princeton University Press, 2007).

SECTION 3
IMPACT

MODULE 9
THE FIRST RESPONSES

KEY POINTS

- Scott's *Gender and the Politics of History* was criticized for its excessive attention to language at the expense of lived experience and material reality.

- Scott responded by arguing that experience of being "female" could not be considered outside of the language in which historical actors themselves made sense of it.

- Despite criticisms, Scott did not fundamentally change her methods.

Criticism

The most immediate responses to Joan Wallach Scott's *Gender and the Politics of History* came mainly from Marxist* scholars and specialists on women's history identified with second-wave feminism.*

From the Marxist camp, the historian Brian Palmer* criticized Scott for "aestheticizing politics" in reference to her use of literary methods. For him poststructuralism*—an understanding of culture and history that questions the existence of objective certainties and the existence of "structures" useful to the analysis of society and literary texts—"denigrates the material as merely representational."[1] There is a suggestion here that Scott studied the *meaning* of experiences rather than *experience itself*, as if nothing existed outside theoretical discussion. Although Palmer agreed with the idea of paying attention to the "master codes of dominant ideologies,"[2] he thought Scott's approach was idealistic and theoretical.

Feminist historians insisted that Scott's methodology was a step backwards because its focus on *representations* of women excluded

" In a 1991 essay, Joan Scott went so far in the direction of particularism as to reject emphatically any 'appeal to experience as uncontestable evidence' in historical research because experience makes ideological systems in any time period appear fixed rather than in constant state of change of mutable identities. This refusal to recognize the objective reality of certain male-inspired dualities and of cognitive male notions about moral and political development, makes it difficult for poststructuralists to focus on the socio-economic and political implications of patriarchy for our own times, let alone the past. "

Joan Hoff, "Response to Joan Scott"

what they considered "real, historical women." Like Palmer, Christine Stansell,* a feminist historian, accused Scott of being an idealist who saw "language as a thing in itself, a pattern of understanding that evolves according to its own internal laws and shapes human experience according to its formal demands."[3] The historian Joan Hoff,* meanwhile, thought that Scott's theory was hostile "to linear change based on causality and the material world,"[4] making historical agency impossible. In other words, Hoff suggested that Scott's theory implied that people were in some way not actually responsible for historical events.

Responses

Scott's initial response to the critics of *Gender* was to insist that they misunderstood the theory she used. She restated that her critics confused "utterances or words" with "discourse."*[5]

Scott took the concept of "discourse" from Michel Foucault.*
According to her interpretation, it meant not merely "ways of thinking,
but ways of organizing lives, institutions, societies," and ways of both
"implementing and justifying inequalities." When she referred to
discourse, she explained, she was not talking about "words" in a literal
sense but to "actions, organizations, institutions, behaviors." For her,
these four elements are "produced in language; they are at once concepts
and practices and need to be analyzed simultaneously as such."[6]

Language, in other words, was *precisely* what makes social experience
intelligible—so perception and experience cannot be separated.
Concepts like the family, for example, are impossible to separate from
actual family relationships, because they appeal "to norms, values,
deeply held beliefs about what was right and wrong, how men and
women ought to behave, who held authority,"[7] and so on.

According to Scott, she was making an argument about gender
and in fact it was her critics who were focused on language. To the
accusation that writing the history of gender left out real, historical
women, Scott responded that people do not arrive at their identities in
a vacuum, with no relation to cultural concepts—so scholars should
understand a woman as she "is constructed and constructs herself,
differentially, in relation to others, men in particular."[8] Assuming an
unmediated identity (that is, one not affected by culture) would
suggest that an essential definition of "woman" was possible. If this
were possible, all women would share the same femininity, decided by
the body that they supposedly had in common.

Scott rejected both this and the views that gender was either
something fixed or a mere reflection of other social relationships such
as politics, class, or economics.[9]

Conflict and Consensus

The early debate about Scott's work, and that of other historians who
embraced poststructuralism and the work of Michel Foucault, almost

became a discussion about the nature of reality and what the legitimate subjects for the study of history might be—a complicated debate without any chance of arriving at one single solution.

As Scott wrote, her critics "shared a fundamental disagreement with my emphasis on 'language,' arguing instead that material reality, social experiences, real or concrete events are the stuff of social history,* while 'language' is ephemeral, epiphenomenal, an 'idealist' preoccupation."[10]

Although early critics did not significantly influence Scott's work, they did prompt many responses from her.[11] Her method remained mostly unchanged and was to become one of the mainstream forms of writing history in American academia over the next 20 years. In the first five to ten years after *Gender and the Politics of History* was published in 1988, critical dialogue was largely focused on Scott's claim that meaning was shaped by language and on how historians could know whether they were studying the past or, in fact, merely language about the past.

Scott did not revise her opinions as a result of criticism. Yet neither was a consensus reached between the different schools of thought debating the issues she had raised.

NOTES

1   Bryan D. Palmer, "Response to Joan Scott," *International Labor and Working-Class History* 31, no. 1 (1987): 153.

2   Palmer, "Response to Joan Scott," 154.

3   Christine Stansell, "A Response to Joan Scott," *International Labor and Working Class History* 31(1987): 27.

4   Joan Hoff, "Gender as a Postmodern Category of Paralysis," *Women's History Review* 3, no. 2 (1994): 151.

5   Joan Wallach Scott, "A Reply to Criticism," *International Labor and Working-Class History*, no. 32 (1987): 39–45, see p. 40.

6   Scott, "A Reply to Criticism," 40.

7   Scott, "A Reply to Criticism," 40.

8   Scott, "A Reply to Criticism," 42.

9   Scott, "A Reply to Criticism," 42.

10 Scott, "A Reply to Criticism," 39.

11 Scott, "A Reply to Criticism," 39–45.

MODULE 10
THE EVOLVING DEBATE

KEY POINTS

- Scott's work was important because it prompted scholars to look at how different categories of analysis interact with each other.

- Gender history emerged as a distinct field in the wake of the publication of *Gender and the Politics of History.*

- Scott's work has had an impact on a variety of different disciplines, ranging from medieval to early-American history.

Uses and Problems

Joan Wallach Scott's *Gender and the Politics of History* was not the only work of its time that attempted to move the study of gender into the mainstream of academic history. Yet it is considered a key text with an expanding influence—especially in its argument that social categories are fluid rather than universal and static.

By encouraging academics to examine the ways in which different categories of analysis interacted with one another—gender, race, ethnicity, nationalism*—the text helped fuel wider debates. It has played a part in prompting scholars to incorporate "post-colonial, critical race,* queer,* and political theory" [1] into their studies. These areas of inquiry are driven, in part, by Scott's idea that gender is a concept created by society to understand and explain sexual difference. As societies change, sexual difference comes to be understood differently. So the concept of gender changes over time and the category itself is worthy of historical study.

❝ I do not think that it is presentist, however, to look back and acknowledge, for example, that Joan Scott's intervention into the discourse wars ended up having a stifling and silencing effect rather than provoking articulate sophisticated responses. **❞**

Mariana Valverde, "Some Remarks on the Rise and Fall of Discourse Analysis"

Women's history now overlaps, and is enriched by, several theoretical schools, reflecting the changing nature of understanding of the historical stability and essential nature of sexuality. Yet Scott's contribution is not without controversy. The Canadian sociologist Mariana Valverde,* for example, has written that "Joan Scott's intervention … ended up having a stifling and silencing effect rather than provoking articulate sophisticated responses."[2]

It should be noted that the intellectual debate has even descended to caricature at times, particularly in the Marxist* opposition to identity politics.* Identity politics is a political movement structured around ideas that prioritize experiences based on cultural, racial, gender, and ethnic commonalities rather than "universal" experiences.[3]

Schools of Thought

Although Scott's *Gender and the Politics of History* has inspired and influenced historians in many disciplines, it is more useful, as Scott herself has insisted, to see her work as part of an ongoing collection of scholarly work concerned with gender.

Caroline Walker Bynum,* a historian of medieval Europe, has contributed to this collection. She published her work during the same period as Scott[4] and revolutionized the field of medieval studies with the first and most influential analysis of gender in the period of her research. Bynum put forward the notion that medieval ideas of "male and female emerge as extremely fragile constructs, mere accidents of heat and moisture, ever-threatening to collapse into one another."[5]

Thanks to the work of scholars like Bynum and Scott, researchers have come to analyze phenomena such as memory, gossip, and emotions through the lens of gender theory. Indeed, scholars have adapted *Gender*'s ideas to other categories of analysis altogether. While historians have used these ideas to explore how gender overlaps with class, race, and ethnicity as categories of analysis, feminists* from developing countries, for example, have insisted that race, gender, and class are interconnected and interdependent categories of domination, more often than not experienced at one and the same time.[6] Recently, gender analysis has offered different insights on topics such as tax law, wage patterns, occupational segregation,* and transfers of wealth between generations.[7]

These scholars have indicated that gender is a useful category for much more than the investigation of the ways in which political power is established—the defining focus of Scott's original analysis.[8]

Scott's theoretical ideas and those of scholars such as Ann Stoler* and G. C. Spivak* have led to what Gary Wilder* describes as "insights about the constitutive power of language or the ways that discourses mediate subjectivity and shape social life"—roughly, the role language plays in creating the world as we understand it. These insights "led some historians to overturn the conventional notions of individuality, intentionality, agency, and causality upon which traditional [methods of writing history] depended."[9]

In Current Scholarship

Scott's *Gender and the Politics of History* is considered one of a number of influential books on the history of gender. It has inspired many historians to follow the avenues of inquiry it opened.

In many parts of academia, the early struggles to establish language and discourse—roughly, the communication of ideas through systems of signs—as legitimate subjects of historical analysis are over. Scott's argument that historical analysis should be conscious of the ways in which language shapes and controls power relationships in society is much more widely accepted than it once was.[10]

We can attribute this to the fact that historians have become increasingly creative, open-minded, and willing to revise and combine methods and sources. If Scott's original intention was to provoke historians to ask questions about categories considered to be either a given or natural—as gender and sex have traditionally been—then the text is often used in ways that are faithful to that aim. Scott explains that there is no "language of gender" whose sole meaning can be understood or measured in scientific fashion. Instead "there are only diverse usages whose meanings must be read. And all that these readings can offer is deeper insight into the history we study, whatever its period or topic."[11]

Efforts to apply Scott's analysis to periods and topics outside of her own era of eighteenth- and nineteenth-century France have included, notably, the work of two medieval scholars, Dyan Elliott* and Caroline Walker Bynum. Both of these thinkers use Scott's text to interpret how categories of gender arise. Elliott has recommended its continued use in the analyses of the power of women as mothers and political figures in medieval history—women such as queens, for example.[12]

As Scott's ideas have spread, scholars have modified gender as a category of analysis. Thanks to historians such as Jeanne Boydston,* a specialist in the early history of North America, its scope now extends beyond that of Scott's study of the power relationships between genders.

NOTES

1   Joanne Meyerowitz, "A History of 'Gender'," *The American Historical Review* 113, no. 5 (2008): 1352.

2   Mariana Valverde, "Some Remarks on the Rise and Fall of Discourse Analysis," *Social History/Histoire Sociale* 33, no. 65 (2000): 75.

3   Eric Hobsbawm, "Identity Politics and the Left," *New Left Review* (1996).

4   Caroline Walker Bynum, *Jesus as Mother: Studies in the Spirituality of the High Middle Ages* (Berkeley: University of California Press, 1984).

5   Dyan Elliott, "The Three Ages of Joan Scott," *The American Historical Review* 113, no. 5 (2008): 1394.

6   For more on this topic see M. B. Zinn and B. T. Dill, "Theorizing Difference from Multiracial Feminism," *Feminist Studies* 22, no. 2 (1996).

7   Alice Kessler-Harris, "A Rich and Adventurous Journey: The Transnational Journey of Gender History in the United States," *Journal of Women's History* 19, no. 1 (2007): 19.

8   Jeanne Boydston, "Gender as a Question of Historical Analysis," *Gender & History* 20, No. 3 (2008): 558–83.

9   Gary Wilder, "From Optic to Topic: The Foreclosure Effect of Historiographic Turns," *The American Historical Review* 117, no. 3 (2012): 726.

10 James W. Cook, "The Kids Are All Right: On the 'Turning' of Cultural History," *American Historical Review* (2012): 746–71.

11 Joan Wallach. Scott, "Unanswered Questions," *The American Historical Review* 113, no. 5 (2008): 1429.

12 Dyan Elliott, "The Three Ages of Joan Scott," *American Historical Review* 13 no. 5 (2008): 1403; see also Gábor Klaniczay, *Holy Rulers and Blessed Princesses: Dynastic Cults in Medieval Central Europe*, trans. Éva Pálmai (Cambridge: Cambridge University Press, 2002).

MODULE 11
IMPACT AND INFLUENCE TODAY

KEY POINTS

- Scott's *Gender and the Politics of History* is still important in challenging the idea that "gender" and "sex" are somehow closely linked.

- Scott's text has pushed historians to include men and masculinity as subjects of analysis in women's history.

- Critics of Scott's work take issue with her political views and have suggested she has tried to indoctrinate her students.

Position

Of the contemporary relevance of her seminal work *Gender and the Politics of History*, Joan Wallach Scott has written: "Gender is about asking historical questions; it is not a programmatic or methodological treatise. It is above all an invitation to think critically about how the meanings of sexed bodies are produced, deployed, and changed; that, finally, is what accounts for its longevity."[1] In other words: why do concepts of gender exist, and why do they persist?

Scott analyzes how language shapes our understanding of gender and the role that politics plays in the creation of power relationships among gender categories. Her work remains relevant to scholars such as historical and comparative sociologists who examine large-scale social change.

The text continues to challenge the assumption that there is some sort of uncomplicated "natural" relationship between gender and sex difference. As Scott explains, the analytical method of deconstruction* "insisted that sex, like gender, had to be understood as a system of

> ** ** Over the last four decades, feminist* scholars have
> contributed immeasurably to our understanding of
> the past, deepening our sense of what history means,
> widening the purview of what history can be, and
> redefining the very categories of historical analysis.
> No one has contributed more in this last sense than
> Joan W. Scott. ** **
>
> *American Historical Review Forum*, "Revisiting 'Gender: A Useful Category of
> Historical Analysis'"

attributed meaning. Neither was about nature; both were products of
culture. Sex was not a transparent phenomenon; it acquired its natural
status retrospectively, as justification for the assignment of gender roles."[2]

For that reason, Scott's theory also challenges any work that does
not treat the concepts of "woman" and "man" as analytical categories
with fluid meanings that alter over time due to political, economic,
and other social changes. Scott's concept "refuses the idea that those
two words transparently describe enduring objects (bodies) and
instead asks how those bodies are thought."[3]

Interaction

In most humanities and social sciences departments in North
American universities, Scott's definition of gender as a linguistically
constructed category is widely (if not uniformly) accepted. Where
there are challenges to her ideas, they are seldom direct. Detractors
usually question Scott's epistemology* (that is, her theoretical
approach to knowledge). Only rarely do they confront her basic
conception of gender.[4]

Encompassing more historical actors, gender history goes beyond
women's history. It includes the study of every historical actor to whom
society ascribed a gender—everyone who ever lived, in other words.

While women's history tended to focus mostly on a narrative about women's experiences in the past and did not analyze how differences between women and men were historically constructed,[5] gender history, according to one scholar, "as the addition of men to the study of women, is more democratic."[6]

It is in the context of this recent work that scholars have begun to write more "rigorously about men as sexed or gendered beings."[7] The past 20 years have seen a large number of studies examining the historical construction of conceptions of masculinity.[8] As Bonnie G. Smith* has written, these studies have led to the "conclusion" that "masculinity—no matter the historical period—was fraught and in crisis."[9]

The Continuing Debate

Gender and the Politics of History is very much part of the current intellectual debate about gender in historical studies.

The response to Scott's work is not coordinated and this reflects the intellectual context of her work. Western academia, especially in the field of history, tends to be multi-faceted and diverse, both in subjects of study and the methodologies that are used to study them.

The motives of those responding to Scott's work are intellectual, professional, and sometimes political. In the 1990s, legitimate intellectual appraisals about method were less visible than political disputes. In the United States, some critics argued that scholars preoccupied with categories such as gender, race, or even class were "radical leftists" who took refuge in academia when the American public began to be unconcerned about "civil rights, anti-war foreign policy, the women's movement, environmental concerns, and countercultural values."[10]

Conservative critics in the US insisted that liberal professors were trying to indoctrinate students. For them "scholarship and ideology could and should be separated," and for this reason they challenged scholars like Scott, who openly admitted their particular political inclinations. Scott's response was that "the production of knowledge is a political enterprise that involves contest among conflicting interests."[11] So to deny the relationship between politics and knowledge was to take a political position while pretending that you were not.

According to Scott, those conservative critics who claimed to be defending tradition and labeled other scholars as "subversive" were using a tactic that allowed them to "present a particular version of culture that gives priority to the writings and viewpoints of European white men, as if it were the only true version, without, however, acknowledging its particularity and exclusiveness. This kind of practice, which discounts and silences the voices and experiences of others, is profoundly undemocratic."[12]

NOTES

1 Joan Wallach. Scott, "Unanswered Questions," *The American Historical Review* 113, no. 5 (2008): 1423.

2 Scott, "Unanswered Questions," 1423.

3 Scott, "Unanswered Questions," 1426.

4 For example, see Bryan D. Palmer, "Response to Joan Scott," *International Labor and Working-Class History* 31, no. 1 (1987): 14–23.

5 Joan Wallach Scott, "A Reply to Criticism," *International Labor and Working-Class History*, no. 32 (1987).

6 Bonnie G. Smith, "Women's History: A Retrospective from the United States," *Signs* 35, no. 3 (2010): 734.

7 Smith, "Women's History," 735.

8 Toby L. Ditz, "The New Men's History and the Peculiar Absence of Gendered Power: Some Remedies from Early American Gender History," *Gender and History* 16 (1): 1–35.

9 Smith, "Women's History," 735.

10 Steven Watts, "The Idiocy of American Studies: Poststructuralism, Language, and Politics in the Age of Self-Fulfilment," *American Quarterly* 43, no. 4 (1991): 631. For more information on the critics of the left in academia see Michael Denning, "The Academic Left and the Rise of Cultural Studies," *Radical History Review* 1992, no. 54 (1992).

11 Joan Wallach Scott, "The Campaign against Political Correctness: What's Really at Stake," *Radical History Review* 1992, no. 54 (1992): 59.

12 Scott, "The Campaign against Political Correctness," 62.

MODULE 12
WHERE NEXT?

KEY POINTS

- Scott still believes that one of the core ideas of *Gender and the Politics of History*, that gender is not defined by a biological idea like "man" or "woman," has not been fully accepted.

- Scott's work is currently having a great impact on the new fields of queer studies* and queer theory.*

- Scott's work has made "gender" a central category of historical analysis.

Potential

Joan Wallach Scott intended her *Gender and the Politics of History* to expand thinking into the role of gender in history. She wanted to uncover the ways in which concepts of gender have developed and changed over time, and how gender has itself influenced society. Although her method was that of the academic historian, her target audience was larger than simply her fellow academics. *Gender* has great potential for interpreting and critiquing the history and politics of gender more broadly.

Feminist* scholars in particular have benefited from Scott's work, and it is likely that the greatest potential for *Gender and the Politics of History* lies in feminist scholarship. If the text has lost any of its relevance, it is precisely due to the explosion of feminist scholarship in the years following the text's initial publication in 1988. The book's ideas have been generally incorporated into the debate.

It should be noted, however, that when Scott wrote the introduction to the second edition of the book, published in 1999, she

> **❝**Joan Scott's work highlights the weakness and strength of queer theory. This book urges that overcoming gender inequality requires two steps: gender visibility and corporeal subjectivity. Likewise Scott proposes a similar process in suggesting that the 'difference dilemma' involves two moves. The first is the systematic criticism of the operations of categorical difference, the exposure of the kinds of exclusions and inclusions—the hierarchies—it constructs. **❞**
>
> Raia Prokhovnik, "Rational Woman: A Feminist Critique of Dichotomy"

lamented that "gender" was still equated by many scholars with "women."[1] Scott indicates that one of the work's key arguments—that gender is a socially constructed concept and is largely distinct from the biological connotations of words like "man" or "woman"—has yet to be fully accepted.

Furthermore, Scott's theoretical contributions to historical studies have potential for further expansion. Her argument that the language of gender is created by society to give meaning to sexual differences still sounds to some historians like an effort to establish radical relativism*—roughly, the idea that since all meaning is decided by society, it is impossible to say what is "real" and what is not.

Future Directions

The core idea of Scott's text—that gender is a concept created by society and that this concept has changed over time—has been developed both by other historians, by activists working for gender equality, and by scholars in recently opened fields such as queer theory.

Queer theory is a method of inquiry that challenges the stable and innate nature of sexuality and relies on similar theoretical foundations to those on which Scott has built her work, particularly poststructuralist* theory. Queer theorists generally share Scott's idea that gender is a social construct,*[2] and have expanded on this initial focus to expose the socially constructed nature of sexual acts and sexual identities.

Although many founding theorists of queer studies initially arrived at their subject from feminism (the gender theorist Judith Butler* among them), since the 1980s theorists have also sought to establish queer studies on an independent footing. In her field-defining article "Thinking Sex," for instance, the cultural anthropologist Gayle Rubin* argued for "an autonomous theory and politics specific to sexuality distinct from a feminist theory of gender oppression."[3] The collection of essays published in 1997 as *Feminism Meets Queer Theory*, edited by the feminist scholar Elizabeth Weed,* meanwhile, attempted to show how feminist and queer theory shared common political interests and intellectual roots.

Summary

Gender and the Politics of History greatly influenced the academic discipline of history, altering the ways in which historians analyze and write about the past. It is now rare for anyone to write about any topic or time period without taking into consideration how conceptions of gender shaped social, political, and economic relationships. Scott—a prominent scholar in her field, even if she is far less well-known outside the academic world—also helped to popularize poststructuralism and the work of the French cultural theorist Michel Foucault* in the field of history. Her approach is now widely used and discussed among many historians.

The author symbolizes the transition from one approach to the writing of history to another. In other words, the change from the social history* that was popular in the 1960s and 1970s to the so-called "linguistic turn,"* a more recent approach that emphasizes theories of language and knowledge.

Although Scott did not invent the concept of gender as a category of historical analysis, she summarized and examined past work about the subject, and adapted it so it could be used to analyze topics beyond traditional women's history.

Noted for the clarity of her analysis, Scott helped to introduce new theoretical traditions to the writing of history, a field that tended to be based on the study of "real world facts" explained through narrative devices.

Gender and the Politics of History is still important. It continues to inspire emerging scholars to consider new ways of analyzing data and sources. Scott popularized the practice of examining discourse* (that is, the ways in which ideas are communicated) through language and conceptions of gender. For her, these are factors that shape everyday life and political developments all over the world. Potentially, the book will continue to be relevant until scholars are less drawn to the persistent inequalities between groups that are justified on the grounds of natural and biological differences.

What sets the ideas introduced in the text apart is Scott's insistence that gender is not peripheral to politics, social layers, or economics, but is central to the way that hierarchies and difference are constructed in society. For Scott, gender permeates every aspect of social life and so deserves special attention. She also helped to debunk the idea that there must be a "universal" historical master narrative—a single true account of events. She pointed out that the stories or symbols framed as universal usually mask particular points of view. Students of history should know, she argues, that "historical knowledge is itself conflictual [and] political" and "certain themes are constructed through the exclusion and suppression of others."[4]

NOTES

1   Joan Wallach Scott, introduction to *Gender and the Politics of History* (New York: Columbia University Press, 1999).

2   Texts significant for queer theory include Judith Butler, *Gender Trouble: Feminism and the Subversion of Identity* (New York: Routledge, 1990) and Eve Kosofsky Sedgwick, *Epistemology of the Closet* (Berkeley: University of California Press, 1990).

3   Lynne Huffer, "Foucault and Feminism's Prodigal Children" in *The Question of Gender: Joan W. Scott's Critical Feminism*, eds. Judith Butler and Elizabeth Weed (Bloomington: Indiana University Press, 2011): 257.

4   Elaine Abelson et al., "Interview with Joan Scott," *Radical History Review* 45 (1989): 50.

GLOSSARY

GLOSSARY OF TERMS

American Historical Association: the oldest and largest association of professional historians in the United States.

Capitalism: an economic system based on private ownership, private enterprise, and the maximization of profit.

Civil Rights Movement: in the United States, a movement mainly of the 1950s and 1960s. Activists and ordinary people came together to stage extensive protests against racial segregation and discrimination.

Cold War: hostilities not involving armed conflict between the forces of the United States and the USSR between approximately 1945 and 1989. It included threats, violent propaganda, espionage, and often the potential of mutual destruction by nuclear weapons.

Communism: an ideal that all citizens in a state should be equal and that the ideal should be imposed by removing markers of difference—such as money, class, and religion—from society. Versions of communism have been used to govern countries across the world, most notably the Soviet Union and China.

Counterculture: the student lifestyles that challenged social norms and expectations in the 1960s, often identified with the youth conflicts in Western Europe around 1968.

Critical race: a field of cultural analysis concerned with issues of race, racism, law, politics, economics, and power.

Critical theory: a body of philosophy with a strong Marxist influence that seeks to critique twentieth- and twenty-first-century society and culture.

Cultural history: a field of history that examines the evolution of popular cultural traditions and provides cultural explanations of historical change.

Deconstruction: a method of linguistic analysis, often used for literary texts, according to which concepts acquire their meaning through their relation to other words and concepts.

Discourse (Foucauldian discourse): French philosopher Michel Foucault's concept of a large system of interrelated signs created through verbal interaction in societies. Discourse is an ever-expanding body of knowledge, articulated in a particular vocabulary, which defines the way in which the world can be "known" and understood.

Division of labor: dividing the component parts of a work task into specific activities to increase efficiency.

Epistemology: a sub-field of philosophy that seeks to understand how knowledge is produced.

Feminism: a movement that seeks to establish political, economic, social, and legal equality for women.

French Revolution of 1848: a revolution that ended the July Monarchy (1830–48) and established the short-lived Second Republic.

Historical materialism: the theory that material factors (technology and modes of economic production) are at the basis of social organization and historical change.

Historiography: the history of a debate as it evolves over time.

Identity politics: a political movement structured around ideas that prioritize experiences based on cultural, racial, gender, and ethnic commonalities rather than "universal" experiences.

Ideology: a set of firmly held beliefs that are used to underpin political and social theories.

Imperialism: "empire-building"; a term generally used for the deliberate extension of a nation's political, cultural, or military influence.

Industrialization: a period of social and economic change characterized by the rise of large-scale means of industrial production.

Labor: work; that part of an industry that requires an individual to perform a physical action.

Liberalization: the relaxation of government restrictions on economic and social activity.

Linguistic turn: a term used to describe a wide range of sometimes-unrelated trends and theories in academia. The idea that unites these theories, in a very simplified form, is that language (or linguistic systems) rather than experience or reality provides the content of our knowledge.

Male–female binary: a system of classification that pits sex and gender into two distinct and oppositional forms of masculine and feminine.

Marxism: an approach to social science based on materialism, history, and class, founded by Karl Marx in the nineteenth century. It views everything as reflective of an eternal class struggle, with the goal of transforming society into a classless utopia (perfect place). Forms of Marxism remain popular today.

Nationalism: the belief in loyalty, often fiercely held, to the identity, culture, economy, and other features of one's nation-state.

New Left: a left-wing movement originating in the 1960s that advocated change on a variety of political and social issues including gay rights, gender roles, and abortion.

Occupational segregation: the unequal distribution of people based on gender across and within occupations.

Patriarchy: a social system in which men hold primary positions of power and influence within a society

Poststructuralism: an understanding of culture and history that questions the existence of objective certainties and the existence of "structures" useful to the analysis of societies and literary texts.

Queer studies: the academic study of sexual diversity and its related issues.

Queer theory: a method of inquiry that takes as its starting point a challenge to the assumption that sexuality is stable and innate.

Relativism: the view that there is no fixed reality, that experience is meaningless, and that all meaning is created by society.

Republican Party: one of the two major United States political parties alongside the Democratic Party. It favors a conservative approach, supporting free market economy and limited government.

Sears: a famous chain of American department stores.

Second-wave feminism: the more political and social current of feminism of the 1960s that followed earlier "first-wave feminism," in which women demanded the vote and equal recognition under the law, and so on.

September 11, 2001 attacks: the coordinated attacks by politically radicalized Islamic terrorists sponsored by al-Qaeda on the World Trade Center and the Pentagon that occurred on September 11, 2001.

Social construct: the theory that human values and preferences, including sexual orientation, are determined by the social and cultural context in which someone lives.

Social history: a field of history that focuses on how economic factors shape the experience of poor and working-class people.

Social theory: a discipline that seeks to develop frameworks for understanding and explaining social phenomena.

Universalism: a philosophical concept with universal applicability.

PEOPLE MENTIONED IN THE TEXT

Judith Butler (b. 1956) is an American philosopher and feminist, and professor in the department of Comparative Literature and the Program of Critical Theory at UC Berkeley. Her significant works include *Gender Trouble* (1990) and *Bodies that Matter: On the Discursive Limits of Sex* (1993).

Jeanne Boydston (1944–2008) was a prominent American historian, whose work focused on women and gender in Early Republican America.

Caroline Walker Bynum (b. 1941) is a professor emerita of medieval history at Columbia University in the United States, whose work has focused on the intersection of spirituality, theology, and the body in the medieval period.

Jacques Derrida (1930–2004) was a French philosopher. He is notable for his work on the theory of signs, "semiotics," and his contribution to poststructuralist thought, particularly the method of literary analysis known as "deconstructionism."

Dyan Elliott (b. 1954) is a professor of medieval history at Northwestern University in the United States. Her work focuses on the interaction of gender, spirituality, and sexuality in Western Europe during the Middle Ages.

Michel Foucault (1926–84) was a French philosopher who held a chair at the Collège de France between 1970 and 1984. His primary interest was in the relationship between power and knowledge.

Diana Fuss (b. 1960) is a professor of English literature at Princeton University. Her significant works include *Essentially Speaking* (1989).

Linda Gordon (b. 1940) is an American feminist and historian, who is currently professor of history at New York University. She has published on the history of birth control and motherhood in twentieth-century America.

Gareth Stedman Jones (b. 1942) is professor of the History of Ideas at Queen Mary College, University of London. His work has focused on the English working-class in the nineteenth century.

Deniz Kandiyoti (b. 1944) is Emeritus Professor in Development Studies at the School of Oriental and African Studies at the University of London. She has published on nationalism, gender, and Islam in the contemporary world.

Joan Hoff (b. 1937) is a professor of history at Montana State University whose work focuses on gender and twentieth-century American politics.

Afsaneh Najmabadi (b. 1946) is Francis Lee Higginson Professor of History and of Studies of Women, Gender, and Sexuality at Harvard University. She is best known for her work on gender in modern Iran.

Oyeronke Oyewumi is a feminist sociologist at Stony Brook University in the United States. She is best known for her work, *The Invention of Women: Making African Sense of Western Gender Discourses* (1997).

Bryan Palmer is a professor of history at Trent University, Canada, whose work focuses on labor and class in Canada and the United States.

Mary Poovey is a professor of English at New York University, whose work focuses on British literature, history, and culture.

Ronald Reagan (1911–2004) was president of the United States from 1981 to 1989.

Denise Riley (b. 1948) is a British poet and philosopher, best known for her writings on motherhood and women in history.

Will Roscoe (b. 1955) is an American scholar and political activist, whose work has focused on homosexuality in non-Western traditions.

Gayle Rubin (b. 1949) is an American cultural anthropologist and professor of Anthropology and Women's Studies at the University of Michigan. She is an activist and a theorist of queer issues, sex, and the politics of gender.

Christine Stansell (b. 1949) is a professor of history at the University of Chicago. Her work focuses on women's and gender history in the pre-Civil War United States.

Ann Stoler (b. 1949) is a professor of anthropology and history at the New School for Social Research in New York City. Her work focuses on race and colonial governance in Southeast Asia.

William Sewell (b. 1940) is a historian, currently Distinguished Service Professor Emeritus of History and Political Science at the University of Chicago. He has made significant contributions to modern French labor, social, cultural, and political history.

Bonnie G. Smith (b. 1940) is a distinguished professor of history at Rutgers University, best known for her pioneering work in women's history and gender history.

G. C. Spivak (b. 1942) is an Indian literary theorist and philosopher at Columbia University, best known for her pioneering essay "Can the Subaltern Speak?"

E. P. Thompson (1924–93) was a historian of social movements in eighteenth- and nineteenth-century Britain, and a leading Marxist figure. His important works include *The Making of the English Working Class* (1963).

Charles Tilly (1929–2008) was an American sociologist who authored groundbreaking studies on state formation and social movements. His significant publications include *From Mobilization to Revolution* (1978) and *Big Structures, Large Processes, Huge Comparisons* (1984).

Louise Tilly (b. 1930) is an American historian whose work is notable for fusing sociology with historical research. Her work has focused on women, work, and family life in nineteenth-century Europe.

Mariana Valverde (b. 1955) is a Canadian sociologist at the University of Toronto. She is currently director and professor of the Centre of Criminology at the University of Toronto.

Elizabeth Weed (b. 1940) is professor of Modern Culture and Media at Brown University and was director of the Pembroke Center for Teaching and Research on Women between 2000 and 2010.

Gary Wilder is associate professor of anthropology at the City University of New York Graduate Center.

WORKS CITED

WORKS CITED

Abelson, Elaine, David Abraham, and Marjorie Murphy. "Interview with Joan Scott." *Radical History Review* 45 (1989): 41–59.

AHR Forum. "Revisiting 'Gender: A Useful Category of Historical Analysis'": Introduction." *American Historical Review* 113, no. 5 (2008): 1344–5.

Balkin, Jack M., and Sanford Levinson. "Law and the Humanities: An Uneasy Relationship." *Daedalus* 135, no. 2 (2006): 105–15.

Belsey, Catherine. *Poststructuralism: A Very Short Introduction*. New York: Oxford University Press, 2002.

Benhabib, Selya. *Situating the Self: Gender, Community and Postmodernism in Contemporary Ethics*. New York: Routledge, 1992.

Berger, M. A., and L. M. Solan. "The Uneasy Relationship between Science and Law: An Essay and Introduction [Symposium: A Cross-Disciplinary Look at Scientific Truth]." *Brooklyn Law Review* 73, no. 3 (2008): 847.

Boydston, Jeanne. "Gender as a Question of Historical Analysis." *Gender & History* 20, no. 3 (2008): 558-83.

Bucur, Maria. "An Archipelago of Stories: Gender History in Eastern Europe." *The American Historical Review* 113, no. 5 (2008): 1375–89.

Butler, Judith. *Gender Trouble: Feminism and the Subversion of Identity*. New York: Routledge, 1990.

Bynum, Caroline Walker. *Jesus as Mother: Studies in the Spirituality of the High Middle Ages*. Berkeley: University of California Press, 1984.

Cook, James W. "The Kids Are All Right: On the 'Turning' of Cultural History." *The American Historical Review* 117, no. 3 (2012): 746–71.

Cooper, Frederick, and Randall M. Packard. *International Development and the Social Sciences Essays on the History and Politics of Knowledge*. Berkeley: University of California Press, 1997.

Denning, Michael. "The Academic Left and the Rise of Cultural Studies." *Radical History Review* 1992, no. 54 (1992): 21–47.

Derrida, Jacques. *Of Grammatology.* Translated by Gayatri Chakravorty Spivak. Baltimore: Johns Hopkins University Press: 1976.

Derrida, Jacques, and John D. Caputo. *Deconstruction in a Nutshell: A Conversation with Jacques Derrida*. New York: Fordham University Press, 1997.

Ditz, Toby L. "The New Men's History and the Peculiar Absence of Gendered Power: Some Remedies from Early American Gender History." *Gender and History* 16 (1): 1–35.

Elliott, Dyan "The Three Ages of Joan Scott." *The American Historical Review* 113, no. 5 (2008): 1390–1403.

Fine, Cordelia. *Delusions of Gender: How Our Minds, Society, and Neurosexism Create Difference*. New York: WW Norton, 2010.

Fuss, Diana. *Essentially Speaking: Feminism, Nature and Difference*. New York: Routledge, 1989.

Gordon, Linda *Heroes of their Own Lives: The Politics and History of Family Violence: Boston 1880–1960*. New York: Viking, 1988.

"Response to Scott," *Signs* 15, vol. 4 (1990): 852–3.

Hershatter, Gail, and Wang Zheng. "Chinese History: A Useful Category of Gender Analysis." *The American Historical Review* 113, no. 5 (2008): 1404–21.

Hobsbawm, Eric. "Identity Politics and the Left." *New Left Review* (1996): 38–47.

Hoff, Joan. "Gender as a Postmodern Category of Paralysis." *Women's History Review* 3, no. 2 (1994): 149–68.

Huffer, Lynne. "Foucault and Feminism's Prodigal Children." In *The Question of Gender: Joan W. Scott's Critical Feminism,* edited by Judith Butler and Elizabeth Weed, 257. Bloomington: Indiana University Press, 2011.

Johnson, Joy L., Lorraine Greaves, and Robin Repta. *Better Science with Sex and Gender: A Primer for Health Research*. Women's Health Research Network, 2007.

Jones, Gareth Stedman. *Languages of Class: Studies in English Working Class History, 1832–1982*. Cambridge; New York: Cambridge University Press, 1983.

Jordan-Young, Rebecca, and Raffaella I. Rumiati. "Hardwired for Sexism? Approaches to Sex/Gender in Neuroscience." *Neuroethics* (2011): 1–11.

Kandiyoti, Deniz. *The Politics of Gender and Reconstruction in Afghanistan*. Geneva: UNRISD, 2005.

Kent, Susan Kingsley "Mistrials and Diatribulations: A Reply to Joan Hoff." *Women's History Review* 5, no. 1 (1996): 9-18.

Kessler-Harris, Alice. "A Rich and Adventurous Journey: The Transnational Journey of Gender History in the United States." *Journal of Women's History* 19, no. 1 (2007): 153–9.

Klaniczay, Gábor. *Holy Rulers and Blessed Princesses: Dynastic Cults in Medieval Central Europe*. Translated by Éva Pálmai. Cambridge: Cambridge University Press, 2002.

Kramer, Lloyd. "The Politics of the Veil by Joan Wallach Scott." *The Journal of Modern History* 81, no. 3 (2009): 700–02.

Meyerowitz, Joanne. "A History of 'Gender'." *The American Historical Review* 113, no. 5 (2008): 1346–56.

Morgan, Sue. "Theorising Feminist History: a Thirty-Year Retrospective." *Women's History Review* 18, no. 3 (2009): 381–407.

Munslow, Alun. *Deconstructing History*. 2nd ed. London: Routledge, 2006

Najmabadi, Afsaneh. "Beyond the Americas." *Journal of Women's History* 18, no. 1 (2006): 11–21.

"Mapping Transformations of Sex, Gender, and Sexuality in Modern Iran." *Social Analysis* 49, no. 2 (2005): 54–77.

O'Connor, Alice. *Poverty Knowledge: Social Science, Social Policy, and the Poor in Twentieth-Century U.S. History*. Princeton, N.J.: Princeton University Press, 2001.

Oyewumi, Oyeronke. "Conceptualizing Gender: The Eurocentric Foundations of Feminist Concepts and the Challenge of African Epistemologies." *Jenda: a Journal of Culture and African Woman Studies* 2 (2002): 1.

Palmer, Bryan D. "Critical Theory, Historical Materialism, and the Ostensible End of Marxism: The Poverty of Theory Revisited." *International Review of Social History* 38. no. 2 (1993): 133–62.

"Response to Joan Scott." *International Labor and Working-Class History* 31, no. 1 (1987): 14–23.

Peck, Jamie, and Nik Theodore. "Recombinant Workfare, across the Americas: Transnationalizing 'Fast' Social Policy." *Geoforum* 41, no. 2 (2010): 195.

Poovey, Mary. *Uneven Developments: The Ideological Work of Gender in mid-Victorian England*. Chicago: University of Chicago Press, 1988.

Prokhovnik, Ria. *Rational Woman: A Feminist Critique of Dichotomy.* Routledge, 1999.

Ricoeur, Paul. *Time and Narrative.* 3 vols. Translated by Kathleen McLaughlin and David Pellauer. Chicago: University of Chicago Press, 1984–8.

Riley, Denise. *"Am I That Name?": Feminism and the Category of "Women" in History*. Minneapolis: University of Minnesota, 1988.

Rose, Sonya O. "Introduction to Dialogue: Gender History/Women's History: Is Feminist Scholarship Losing Its Critical Edge?" *Journal of Women's History* 5, no. 1 (1993): 89–128.

Scott, Joan Wallach. "The Campaign against Political Correctness: What's Really at Stake." *Radical History Review* 1992, no. 54 (1992): 59–79.

"The 'Class' We Have Lost." *International Labor and Working-Class History* 57 (2000): 69–75.

"Deconstructing Equality-Versus-Difference: Or, the Uses of Poststructuralist Theory for Feminism." *Feminist Studies* 14, no. 1 (1988): 32–50.

"Deconstructing Equality-Versus-Difference: Or, the Uses of Poststructuralist Theory for Feminism." In *The Postmodern Turn: New Perspectives on Social Theory*, edited by Steve Seidman, 282–98: Cambridge University Press, 1994.

Gender and the Politics of History. New York: Columbia University Press, 1999.

"Gender: A Useful Category of Historical Analysis." *American Historical Review* 91 (1986).

"Middle East Studies Under Attack." *The Link* 39, no. 1 (2006): 2–13.

"Multiculturalism and the Politics of Identity." *October* 61 (1992): 12–19.

Only Paradoxes to Offer: French Feminists and the Rights of Man. Cambridge, MA: Harvard University Press, 1996.

Parité! Sexual Equality and the Crisis of French Universalism. Chicago: University of Chicago Press, 2005.

The Politics of the Veil. Princeton, NJ: Princeton University Press, 2007.

"A Reply to Criticism." *International Labor and Working-Class History*, no. 32 (1987): 39–45.

"Response to Review on *Gender and the Politics of History*." *Signs* 15, no. 4 (1990): 859–60.

"Unanswered Questions." *The American Historical Review* 113, no. 5 (2008): 1422–30.

Scott, Joan Wallach, and Louise A. Tilly. *Women, Work, and Family.* New York: Holt, Reinhart and Winston, 1978.

Sedgwick, Eve Kosofsky. *Epistemology of the Closet.* Berkeley: University of California Press, 1990.

Sewell, William H. *Logics of History: Social Theory and Social Transformation*: University of Chicago Press, 2005.

Smith, Bonnie G. "Women's History: A Retrospective from the United States." *Signs* 35, no. 3 (2010): 723–47.

Spiegel, Gabrielle M. "The Task of the Historian." *The American Historical Review* 114, no. 1 (2009): 1–15.

Springer, Kristen W., Jeanne Mager Stellman, and Rebecca M. Jordan-Young. "Beyond a Catalogue of Differences: A Theoretical Frame and Good Practice Guidelines for Researching Sex/Gender in Human Health." *Social Science & Medicine* 74, no. 11 (2012): 1817–24.

Stansell, Christine. "A Response to Joan Scott." *International Labor and Working Class History* 31 (1987): 28.

Stoler, Ann Laura. *Race and the Education of Desire: Foucault's History of Sexuality and the Colonial Order of Things*. Durham: Duke University Press, 1995.

Surkis, Judith. "When Was the Linguistic Turn? A Genealogy." *The American Historical Review* 117, no. 3 (2012): 700–22.

Thompson, E. P. *The Making of the English Working Class*. London: Gollancz, 1963.

The Poverty of Theory & Other Essays. New York: Monthly Review Press, 1978.

Tinsman, Heidi. "A Paradigm of Our Own: Joan Scott in Latin American History." *The American Historical Review* 113, no. 5 (2008): 1357–74.

True, Jacqui, and Michael Mintrom. "Transnational Networks and Policy Diffusion: The Case of Gender Mainstreaming." *International Studies Quarterly* 45, no. 1 (2001): 27–57.

United Nations General Assembly, Sixty-Fourth Session. "Resolution 64/289, (A/RES/64/289)." New York, July 2, 2010.

United Nations Economic and Social Council, "Report on the Fifty-Fourth Session (E.CN.6.2010/11)." *Commission on the Status of Women.* New York, 2010.

UN Women. "UN Women Annual Report 2011–2012." *United Nations Entity for Gender Equality and the Empowerment of Women.* New York, 2012.

Valverde, Mariana. "Some Remarks on the Rise and Fall of Discourse Analysis." *Social History/Histoire Sociale* 33, no. 65 (2000).

Watts, Steven. "The Idiocy of American Studies: Poststructuralism, Language, and Politics in the Age of Self-Fulfilment." *American Quarterly* 43, no. 4 (1991): 625–60.

Wilder, Gary. "From Optic to Topic: The Foreclosure Effect of Historiographic Turns." *The American Historical Review* 117, no. 3 (2012): 723–45.

World Bank. "World Development Report 2012: Gender Equality and Development." *The International Bank for Reconstruction and Development*. Washington, DC, 2012.

Zinn, M. B., and B.T. Dill. "Theorizing Difference from Multiracial Feminism." *Feminist Studies* 22, no. 2 (1996): 321–31.

Zipp, John F., and Rudy Fenwick. "Is the Academy a Liberal Hegemony? The Political Orientations and Educational Values of Professors." *Public Opinion Quarterly* 70, no. 3 (2006): 304–26.

THE MACAT LIBRARY
BY DISCIPLINE

AFRICANA STUDIES

Chinua Achebe's *An Image of Africa: Racism in Conrad's Heart of Darkness*
W. E. B. Du Bois's *The Souls of Black Folk*
Zora Neale Huston's *Characteristics of Negro Expression*
Martin Luther King Jr's *Why We Can't Wait*
Toni Morrison's *Playing in the Dark: Whiteness in the American Literary Imagination*

ANTHROPOLOGY

Arjun Appadurai's *Modernity at Large: Cultural Dimensions of Globalisation*
Philippe Ariès's *Centuries of Childhood*
Franz Boas's *Race, Language and Culture*
Kim Chan & Renée Mauborgne's *Blue Ocean Strategy*
Jared Diamond's *Guns, Germs & Steel: the Fate of Human Societies*
Jared Diamond's *Collapse: How Societies Choose to Fail or Survive*
E. E. Evans-Pritchard's *Witchcraft, Oracles and Magic Among the Azande*
James Ferguson's *The Anti-Politics Machine*
Clifford Geertz's *The Interpretation of Cultures*
David Graeber's *Debt: the First 5000 Years*
Karen Ho's *Liquidated: An Ethnography of Wall Street*
Geert Hofstede's *Culture's Consequences: Comparing Values, Behaviors, Institutes and Organizations across Nations*
Claude Lévi-Strauss's *Structural Anthropology*
Jay Macleod's *Ain't No Makin' It: Aspirations and Attainment in a Low-Income Neighborhood*
Saba Mahmood's *The Politics of Piety: The Islamic Revival and the Feminist Subject*
Marcel Mauss's *The Gift*

BUSINESS

Jean Lave & Etienne Wenger's *Situated Learning*
Theodore Levitt's *Marketing Myopia*
Burton G. Malkiel's *A Random Walk Down Wall Street*
Douglas McGregor's *The Human Side of Enterprise*
Michael Porter's *Competitive Strategy: Creating and Sustaining Superior Performance*
John Kotter's *Leading Change*
C. K. Prahalad & Gary Hamel's *The Core Competence of the Corporation*

CRIMINOLOGY

Michelle Alexander's *The New Jim Crow: Mass Incarceration in the Age of Colorblindness*
Michael R. Gottfredson & Travis Hirschi's *A General Theory of Crime*
Richard Herrnstein & Charles A. Murray's *The Bell Curve: Intelligence and Class Structure in American Life*
Elizabeth Loftus's *Eyewitness Testimony*
Jay Macleod's *Ain't No Makin' It: Aspirations and Attainment in a Low-Income Neighborhood*
Philip Zimbardo's *The Lucifer Effect*

ECONOMICS

Janet Abu-Lughod's *Before European Hegemony*
Ha-Joon Chang's *Kicking Away the Ladder*
David Brion Davis's *The Problem of Slavery in the Age of Revolution*
Milton Friedman's *The Role of Monetary Policy*
Milton Friedman's *Capitalism and Freedom*
David Graeber's *Debt: the First 5000 Years*
Friedrich Hayek's *The Road to Serfdom*
Karen Ho's *Liquidated: An Ethnography of Wall Street*

John Maynard Keynes's *The General Theory of Employment, Interest and Money*
Charles P. Kindleberger's *Manias, Panics and Crashes*
Robert Lucas's *Why Doesn't Capital Flow from Rich to Poor Countries?*
Burton G. Malkiel's *A Random Walk Down Wall Street*
Thomas Robert Malthus's *An Essay on the Principle of Population*
Karl Marx's *Capital*
Thomas Piketty's *Capital in the Twenty-First Century*
Amartya Sen's *Development as Freedom*
Adam Smith's *The Wealth of Nations*
Nassim Nicholas Taleb's *The Black Swan: The Impact of the Highly Improbable*
Amos Tversky's & Daniel Kahneman's *Judgment under Uncertainty: Heuristics and Biases*
Mahbub Ul Haq's *Reflections on Human Development*
Max Weber's *The Protestant Ethic and the Spirit of Capitalism*

FEMINISM AND GENDER STUDIES

Judith Butler's *Gender Trouble*
Simone De Beauvoir's *The Second Sex*
Michel Foucault's *History of Sexuality*
Betty Friedan's *The Feminine Mystique*
Saba Mahmood's *The Politics of Piety: The Islamic Revival and the Feminist Subjec*t
Joan Wallach Scott's *Gender and the Politics of History*
Mary Wollstonecraft's *A Vindication of the Rights of Woman*
Virginia Woolf's *A Room of One's Own*

GEOGRAPHY

The Brundtland Report's *Our Common Future*
Rachel Carson's *Silent Spring*
Charles Darwin's *On the Origin of Species*
James Ferguson's *The Anti-Politics Machine*
Jane Jacobs's *The Death and Life of Great American Cities*
James Lovelock's *Gaia: A New Look at Life on Earth*
Amartya Sen's *Development as Freedom*
Mathis Wackernagel & William Rees's *Our Ecological Footprint*

HISTORY

Janet Abu-Lughod's *Before European Hegemony*
Benedict Anderson's *Imagined Communities*
Bernard Bailyn's *The Ideological Origins of the American Revolution*
Hanna Batatu's *The Old Social Classes And The Revolutionary Movements Of Iraq*
Christopher Browning's *Ordinary Men: Reserve Police Batallion 101 and the Final Solution in Poland*
Edmund Burke's *Reflections on the Revolution in France*
William Cronon's *Nature's Metropolis: Chicago And The Great West*
Alfred W. Crosby's *The Columbian Exchange*
Hamid Dabashi's *Iran: A People Interrupted*
David Brion Davis's *The Problem of Slavery in the Age of Revolution*
Nathalie Zemon Davis's *The Return of Martin Guerre*
Jared Diamond's *Guns, Germs & Steel: the Fate of Human Societies*
Frank Dikotter's *Mao's Great Famine*
John W Dower's *War Without Mercy: Race And Power In The Pacific War*
W. E. B. Du Bois's *The Souls of Black Folk*
Richard J. Evans's *In Defence of History*
Lucien Febvre's *The Problem of Unbelief in the 16th Century*
Sheila Fitzpatrick's *Everyday Stalinism*

The Macat Library By Discipline

Eric Foner's *Reconstruction: America's Unfinished Revolution, 1863-1877*
Michel Foucault's *Discipline and Punish*
Michel Foucault's *History of Sexuality*
Francis Fukuyama's *The End of History and the Last Man*
John Lewis Gaddis's *We Now Know: Rethinking Cold War History*
Ernest Gellner's *Nations and Nationalism*
Eugene Genovese's *Roll, Jordan, Roll: The World the Slaves Made*
Carlo Ginzburg's *The Night Battles*
Daniel Goldhagen's *Hitler's Willing Executioners*
Jack Goldstone's *Revolution and Rebellion in the Early Modern World*
Antonio Gramsci's *The Prison Notebooks*
Alexander Hamilton, John Jay & James Madison's *The Federalist Papers*
Christopher Hill's *The World Turned Upside Down*
Carole Hillenbrand's *The Crusades: Islamic Perspectives*
Thomas Hobbes's *Leviathan*
Eric Hobsbawm's *The Age Of Revolution*
John A. Hobson's *Imperialism: A Study*
Albert Hourani's *History of the Arab Peoples*
Samuel P. Huntington's *The Clash of Civilizations and the Remaking of World Order*
C. L. R. James's *The Black Jacobins*
Tony Judt's *Postwar: A History of Europe Since 1945*
Ernst Kantorowicz's *The King's Two Bodies: A Study in Medieval Political Theology*
Paul Kennedy's *The Rise and Fall of the Great Powers*
Ian Kershaw's *The "Hitler Myth": Image and Reality in the Third Reich*
John Maynard Keynes's *The General Theory of Employment, Interest and Money*
Charles P. Kindleberger's *Manias, Panics and Crashes*
Martin Luther King Jr's *Why We Can't Wait*
Henry Kissinger's *World Order: Reflections on the Character of Nations and the Course of History*
Thomas Kuhn's *The Structure of Scientific Revolutions*
Georges Lefebvre's *The Coming of the French Revolution*
John Locke's *Two Treatises of Government*
Niccolò Machiavelli's *The Prince*
Thomas Robert Malthus's *An Essay on the Principle of Population*
Mahmood Mamdani's *Citizen and Subject: Contemporary Africa And The Legacy Of Late Colonialism*
Karl Marx's *Capital*
Stanley Milgram's *Obedience to Authority*
John Stuart Mill's *On Liberty*
Thomas Paine's *Common Sense*
Thomas Paine's *Rights of Man*
Geoffrey Parker's *Global Crisis: War, Climate Change and Catastrophe in the Seventeenth Century*
Jonathan Riley-Smith's *The First Crusade and the Idea of Crusading*
Jean-Jacques Rousseau's *The Social Contract*
Joan Wallach Scott's *Gender and the Politics of History*
Theda Skocpol's *States and Social Revolutions*
Adam Smith's *The Wealth of Nations*
Timothy Snyder's *Bloodlands: Europe Between Hitler and Stalin*
Sun Tzu's *The Art of War*
Keith Thomas's *Religion and the Decline of Magic*
Thucydides's *The History of the Peloponnesian War*
Frederick Jackson Turner's *The Significance of the Frontier in American History*
Odd Arne Westad's *The Global Cold War: Third World Interventions And The Making Of Our Times*

LITERATURE

Chinua Achebe's *An Image of Africa: Racism in Conrad's Heart of Darkness*
Roland Barthes's *Mythologies*
Homi K. Bhabha's *The Location of Culture*
Judith Butler's *Gender Trouble*
Simone De Beauvoir's *The Second Sex*
Ferdinand De Saussure's *Course in General Linguistics*
T. S. Eliot's *The Sacred Wood: Essays on Poetry and Criticism*
Zora Neale Huston's *Characteristics of Negro Expression*
Toni Morrison's *Playing in the Dark: Whiteness in the American Literary Imagination*
Edward Said's *Orientalism*
Gayatri Chakravorty Spivak's *Can the Subaltern Speak?*
Mary Wollstonecraft's *A Vindication of the Rights of Women*
Virginia Woolf's *A Room of One's Own*

PHILOSOPHY

Elizabeth Anscombe's *Modern Moral Philosophy*
Hannah Arendt's *The Human Condition*
Aristotle's *Metaphysics*
Aristotle's *Nicomachean Ethics*
Edmund Gettier's *Is Justified True Belief Knowledge?*
Georg Wilhelm Friedrich Hegel's *Phenomenology of Spirit*
David Hume's *Dialogues Concerning Natural Religion*
David Hume's *The Enquiry for Human Understanding*
Immanuel Kant's *Religion within the Boundaries of Mere Reason*
Immanuel Kant's *Critique of Pure Reason*
Søren Kierkegaard's *The Sickness Unto Death*
Søren Kierkegaard's *Fear and Trembling*
C. S. Lewis's *The Abolition of Man*
Alasdair MacIntyre's *After Virtue*
Marcus Aurelius's *Meditations*
Friedrich Nietzsche's *On the Genealogy of Morality*
Friedrich Nietzsche's *Beyond Good and Evil*
Plato's *Republic*
Plato's *Symposium*
Jean-Jacques Rousseau's *The Social Contract*
Gilbert Ryle's *The Concept of Mind*
Baruch Spinoza's *Ethics*
Sun Tzu's *The Art of War*
Ludwig Wittgenstein's *Philosophical Investigations*

POLITICS

Benedict Anderson's *Imagined Communities*
Aristotle's *Politics*
Bernard Bailyn's *The Ideological Origins of the American Revolution*
Edmund Burke's *Reflections on the Revolution in France*
John C. Calhoun's *A Disquisition on Government*
Ha-Joon Chang's *Kicking Away the Ladder*
Hamid Dabashi's *Iran: A People Interrupted*
Hamid Dabashi's *Theology of Discontent: The Ideological Foundation of the Islamic Revolution in Iran*
Robert Dahl's *Democracy and its Critics*
Robert Dahl's *Who Governs?*
David Brion Davis's *The Problem of Slavery in the Age of Revolution*

The Macat Library By Discipline

Alexis De Tocqueville's *Democracy in America*
James Ferguson's *The Anti-Politics Machine*
Frank Dikotter's *Mao's Great Famine*
Sheila Fitzpatrick's *Everyday Stalinism*
Eric Foner's *Reconstruction: America's Unfinished Revolution, 1863-1877*
Milton Friedman's *Capitalism and Freedom*
Francis Fukuyama's *The End of History and the Last Man*
John Lewis Gaddis's *We Now Know: Rethinking Cold War History*
Ernest Gellner's *Nations and Nationalism*
David Graeber's *Debt: the First 5000 Years*
Antonio Gramsci's *The Prison Notebooks*
Alexander Hamilton, John Jay & James Madison's *The Federalist Papers*
Friedrich Hayek's *The Road to Serfdom*
Christopher Hill's *The World Turned Upside Down*
Thomas Hobbes's *Leviathan*
John A. Hobson's *Imperialism: A Study*
Samuel P. Huntington's *The Clash of Civilizations and the Remaking of World Order*
Tony Judt's *Postwar: A History of Europe Since 1945*
David C. Kang's *China Rising: Peace, Power and Order in East Asia*
Paul Kennedy's *The Rise and Fall of Great Powers*
Robert Keohane's *After Hegemony*
Martin Luther King Jr.'s *Why We Can't Wait*
Henry Kissinger's *World Order: Reflections on the Character of Nations and the Course of History*
John Locke's *Two Treatises of Government*
Niccolò Machiavelli's *The Prince*
Thomas Robert Malthus's *An Essay on the Principle of Population*
Mahmood Mamdani's *Citizen and Subject: Contemporary Africa And The Legacy Of Late Colonialism*
Karl Marx's *Capital*
John Stuart Mill's *On Liberty*
John Stuart Mill's *Utilitarianism*
Hans Morgenthau's *Politics Among Nations*
Thomas Paine's *Common Sense*
Thomas Paine's *Rights of Man*
Thomas Piketty's *Capital in the Twenty-First Century*
Robert D. Putnam's *Bowling Alone*
John Rawls's *Theory of Justice*
Jean-Jacques Rousseau's *The Social Contract*
Theda Skocpol's *States and Social Revolutions*
Adam Smith's *The Wealth of Nations*
Sun Tzu's *The Art of War*
Henry David Thoreau's *Civil Disobedience*
Thucydides's *The History of the Peloponnesian War*
Kenneth Waltz's *Theory of International Politics*
Max Weber's *Politics as a Vocation*
Odd Arne Westad's *The Global Cold War: Third World Interventions And The Making Of Our Times*

POSTCOLONIAL STUDIES

Roland Barthes's *Mythologies*
Frantz Fanon's *Black Skin, White Masks*
Homi K. Bhabha's *The Location of Culture*
Gustavo Gutiérrez's *A Theology of Liberation*
Edward Said's *Orientalism*
Gayatri Chakravorty Spivak's *Can the Subaltern Speak?*

PSYCHOLOGY

Gordon Allport's *The Nature of Prejudice*
Alan Baddeley & Graham Hitch's *Aggression: A Social Learning Analysis*
Albert Bandura's *Aggression: A Social Learning Analysis*
Leon Festinger's *A Theory of Cognitive Dissonance*
Sigmund Freud's *The Interpretation of Dreams*
Betty Friedan's *The Feminine Mystique*
Michael R. Gottfredson & Travis Hirschi's *A General Theory of Crime*
Eric Hoffer's *The True Believer: Thoughts on the Nature of Mass Movements*
William James's *Principles of Psychology*
Elizabeth Loftus's *Eyewitness Testimony*
A. H. Maslow's *A Theory of Human Motivation*
Stanley Milgram's *Obedience to Authority*
Steven Pinker's *The Better Angels of Our Nature*
Oliver Sacks's *The Man Who Mistook His Wife For a Hat*
Richard Thaler & Cass Sunstein's *Nudge: Improving Decisions About Health, Wealth and Happiness*
Amos Tversky's *Judgment under Uncertainty: Heuristics and Biases*
Philip Zimbardo's *The Lucifer Effect*

SCIENCE

Rachel Carson's *Silent Spring*
William Cronon's *Nature's Metropolis: Chicago And The Great West*
Alfred W. Crosby's *The Columbian Exchange*
Charles Darwin's *On the Origin of Species*
Richard Dawkin's *The Selfish Gene*
Thomas Kuhn's *The Structure of Scientific Revolutions*
Geoffrey Parker's *Global Crisis: War, Climate Change and Catastrophe in the Seventeenth Century*
Mathis Wackernagel & William Rees's *Our Ecological Footprint*

SOCIOLOGY

Michelle Alexander's *The New Jim Crow: Mass Incarceration in the Age of Colorblindness*
Gordon Allport's *The Nature of Prejudice*
Albert Bandura's *Aggression: A Social Learning Analysis*
Hanna Batatu's *The Old Social Classes And The Revolutionary Movements Of Iraq*
Ha-Joon Chang's *Kicking Away the Ladder*
W. E. B. Du Bois's *The Souls of Black Folk*
Émile Durkheim's *On Suicide*
Frantz Fanon's *Black Skin, White Masks*
Frantz Fanon's *The Wretched of the Earth*
Eric Foner's *Reconstruction: America's Unfinished Revolution, 1863-1877*
Eugene Genovese's *Roll, Jordan, Roll: The World the Slaves Made*
Jack Goldstone's *Revolution and Rebellion in the Early Modern World*
Antonio Gramsci's *The Prison Notebooks*
Richard Herrnstein & Charles A Murray's *The Bell Curve: Intelligence and Class Structure in American Life*
Eric Hoffer's *The True Believer: Thoughts on the Nature of Mass Movements*
Jane Jacobs's *The Death and Life of Great American Cities*
Robert Lucas's *Why Doesn't Capital Flow from Rich to Poor Countries?*
Jay Macleod's *Ain't No Makin' It: Aspirations and Attainment in a Low Income Neighborhood*
Elaine May's *Homeward Bound: American Families in the Cold War Era*
Douglas McGregor's *The Human Side of Enterprise*
C. Wright Mills's *The Sociological Imagination*

Thomas Piketty's *Capital in the Twenty-First Century*
Robert D. Putman's *Bowling Alone*
David Riesman's *The Lonely Crowd: A Study of the Changing American Character*
Edward Said's *Orientalism*
Joan Wallach Scott's *Gender and the Politics of History*
Theda Skocpol's *States and Social Revolutions*
Max Weber's *The Protestant Ethic and the Spirit of Capitalism*

THEOLOGY

Augustine's *Confessions*
Benedict's *Rule of St Benedict*
Gustavo Gutiérrez's *A Theology of Liberation*
Carole Hillenbrand's *The Crusades: Islamic Perspectives*
David Hume's *Dialogues Concerning Natural Religion*
Immanuel Kant's *Religion within the Boundaries of Mere Reason*
Ernst Kantorowicz's *The King's Two Bodies: A Study in Medieval Political Theology*
Søren Kierkegaard's *The Sickness Unto Death*
C. S. Lewis's *The Abolition of Man*
Saba Mahmood's *The Politics of Piety: The Islamic Revival and the Feminist Subject*
Baruch Spinoza's *Ethics*
Keith Thomas's *Religion and the Decline of Magic*

COMING SOON

Chris Argyris's *The Individual and the Organisation*
Seyla Benhabib's *The Rights of Others*
Walter Benjamin's *The Work Of Art in the Age of Mechanical Reproduction*
John Berger's *Ways of Seeing*
Pierre Bourdieu's *Outline of a Theory of Practice*
Mary Douglas's *Purity and Danger*
Roland Dworkin's *Taking Rights Seriously*
James G. March's *Exploration and Exploitation in Organisational Learning*
Ikujiro Nonaka's *A Dynamic Theory of Organizational Knowledge Creation*
Griselda Pollock's *Vision and Difference*
Amartya Sen's *Inequality Re-Examined*
Susan Sontag's *On Photography*
Yasser Tabbaa's *The Transformation of Islamic Art*
Ludwig von Mises's *Theory of Money and Credit*

Printed in the United States
by Baker & Taylor Publisher Services